BUILDING MAINT

BUILDING MAINTENANCE

A Management Manual

DEREK MILES and PAUL SYAGGA

Prepared for the International Labour Office within the framework of the Construction Management Programme
INTERMEDIATE TECHNOLOGY PUBLICATIONS 1987

Published by Intermediate Technology Publications Ltd
9 King Street, London WC2E 8HW, UK

This edition © the International Labour Organisation 1987

This publication is an expanded version of a *Manual on Building Maintenance* originally published in two volumes © Intermediate Technology Publications in 1976 and 1979.

ISBN 0 946688 92 3

Printed in Great Britain by A. Wheaton & Co. Ltd., Exeter

Contents

Acknowledgements

This manual is based on two previous volumes which were written by Derek Miles and first published by Intermediate Technology Publications Ltd. under the title *A Manual on Building Maintenance* in 1976. The present manual contains a considerable amount of new material on policy aspects and maintenance economics and procedures, resulting from research led by Paul Syagga at the University of Nairobi.

This new revised and expanded edition of the publication was prepared by Derek Miles, Director of Construction Management Programmes in the ILO Management Development Branch, in close collaboration with Paul Syagga, Director of the Housing Research and Development Unit. The manual was prepared as a result of a technical co-operation project funded by the Swedish International Development Authority (SIDA) whose assistance is gratefully acknowledged.

Introduction

As every householder knows, property can be a source of concern as well as a measure of wealth. Time, effort and money must be expended regularly if a building is to maintain its value and provide its occupiers with a satisfactory environment. The task obviously demands technical skills, but even on this micro scale some management must be involved if the work is to be planned and implemented economically and effectively. As the scale moves from micro to macro, so the problems multiply. Maintenance budgets are easy to cut in times of financial stringency. The limited funds available are usually directed towards new buildings rather than the upkeep of existing structures, with the result that the maintenance manager is faced with a growing portfolio of responsibilities but diminishing resources.

Fortunately, there is a growing awareness that maintenance has been overlooked and neglected for too long and that maintenance expenditure should be accepted as an investment which can show a real and attractive economic return. Such a return will only be realized, however, if the maintenance function is properly managed.

Just as maintenance expenditure has been neglected, so has the development of management skills among those involved in maintenance at all levels. The problem is particularly acute in developing countries, where designers, managers and users have no guide-lines to assist them in improving their skills and appreciating their roles in property management in general, and building maintenance in particular.

This manual on the practice of building maintenance has been written to assist policy-makers, managers and supervisors in central government, local authorities, parastatal organizations and private firms. It is also directed towards contractors specializing in maintenance, as well as training and research institutions concerned with building maintenance. It is hoped that the book will encourage greater interest in this neglected area among designers and others who influence the size and nature of maintenance needs; it is also aimed at architectural and engineering students who wish to take a broad view of their future responsibilities.

The manual is divided into three sections: maintenance strategy; maintenance management and maintenance methods. The first section discusses the basis of decision-making in the use of resources for the acquisition and preservation of capital assets. The key issues are the need for a building maintenance policy; the relationship between initial expenditure and running costs and the criteria to be adopted in determining the level of maintenance required for various classes of property. The second section presents a systematic approach to the management of building maintenance, including guide-lines for a system of budgeting and financial control and practical advice on administrative procedures for the management of building maintenance. The third section discusses how to approach the technology of building maintenance, starting with the role of design in minimizing maintenance problems, and progressing to the technical issues of diagnosing maintenance problems and finding remedies.

This book does not pretend to offer a panacea for all building maintenance problems. The authors therefore ask the reader to read it in the light of his or her personal knowledge of local conditions. It is also recognized that both needs and priorities are subject to change, and therefore individual approaches to maintenance management should be sufficiently flexible to adapt to changing technological and socio-economic needs.

DEREK MILES and PAUL SYAGGA
Geneva, 1987

PART ONE
STRATEGY

CHAPTER 1

The Need for a Building Maintenance Policy

A casual stroll around a city, town or village in almost any developing country today suggests that many important national capital assets, such as school buildings, roads, residential houses and apartments, hospitals and civic buildings, are run-down beyond the point of economic repair. Why should this be, when building maintenance is known to be among the most labour-intensive of construction activities? A complete answer has yet to be found but it seems that three main failings are at the root of most of the problems: inadequate finance, bad management and poor building design.

Inadequate finance
It is generally acknowledged that inadequate finance is a major constraint on effective property management, partly because maintenance budgets are the easiest to cut when money is scarce. This book is dedicated to the less obvious proposition that other factors such as poor management and organization or inappropriate design decisions may be even more significant causes of maintenance problems. Nevertheless, there is a limit beyond which maintenance budgets cannot be cut if the building is to provide an efficient and acceptable operating environment to the user.

Maintenance expenditure can be absorbed more easily in commercial and industrial organizations where its costs may account for as little as 0.5 per cent of turnover, but even in these cases maintenance is taken for granted except when it threatens production or profitability. The situation is more serious in the public sector where the damaging effects of poor maintenance are less immediately obvious. In the case of housing estates, it is common for organizations to emphasize the provision of new houses, with little funding provided for maintaining existing stock. Not only are day to day repairs neglected, but efforts at improvements and rehabilitation are considered to be a lower priority than new construction. This is despite the fact that few governments are in a position to provide new housing at a rate which matches the formation of new households. Indeed, the

3

rapid deterioration of existing stock increases the demand for new housing because poorly maintained houses are not only unpopular; they soon reach the stage where the structure itself deteriorates and rebuilding has to be considered.

It would be wrong to blame policy-makers and officials in operational ministries for this state of affairs, since they cannot allocate funds if no funds are available. Thus the roles of national treasuries, financing and donor agencies must also be considered. It is usually much easier to secure finance for new infrastructure than for projects aimed at ensuring the adequate maintenance of existing structures. Perhaps the accountant's somewhat arbitrary distinction between capital and recurrent expenditure is the true culprit, although an additional factor is the prestige attached to new projects *vis-à-vis* the mundane problems of maintenance. Some of the more progressive agencies are already reviewing their policy on maintenance projects, and it is hoped that others will become more receptive to approaches for projects aimed at ensuring that existing investments are protected and continue to yield the benefits they were designed to provide.

Bad management
Bad management may be simply a reflection of idleness and waste among maintenance personnel but there is usually much more to it than that. Is maintenance a planned activity, or does the manager simply react to the most immediate crisis? There can be no doubt that building maintenance is an aspect of construction management which is susceptible to considerable improvements in performance through the introduction of effective management procedures. Indeed, since planned maintenance can be seen as a form of 'steady state' activity, while project management frequently deals in one-off projects for which there is no precedent, the management of building maintenance should be relatively easy (the word 'relatively' is used advisedly!). However, it has been woefully neglected: Part 2 of this book attempts to provide some basic tools to show the maintenance manager how to exercise more effective control over his activities.

Poor building design
It is not uncommon to find that buildings are inherently expensive to maintain on account of inappropriate priorities applied during the design phase. Poor detailing and the specification of unsuitable components and materials are common

complaints. In addition, construction errors arising from inadequate drawings and specifications, coupled with poor workmanship because of contracts awarded to incompetent contractors are frequent causes of rapid physical deterioration in buildings. Good design should allow accessibility and adequate working space for essential maintenance such as cleaning, and minor repairs to pipes, ducts and cables. The use of flexible connections or slide-and-glue joints can also be helpful. The relationship between maintenance and building design is the subject of Chapter 8.

Functional obsolescence
Inappropriate building design may also lead to functional obsolescence. This occurs, for instance, when rooms are too small, ceilings too high, natural light is inadequate, or the architectural plan, style and design are poor. The designer may also fail to consider appropriately the socio-cultural factors pertaining to the needs of the user, particularly in the case of housing estates. All the factors inherent in the structural layout and materials which are responsible for depreciation or decrease in the value of a building may be classified as functional obsolescence. This is a separate factor from 'economic obsolescence' which is a loss in value resulting from conditions outside the building, for example proximity to a new airport, or adverse legislation from the property owner's point of view such as rent control, or factory closures leading to a loss of employment opportunities.

The net result of functional obsolescence is that large sums of money may have to be spent on improvements or rehabilitation to bring a building back to a satisfactory standard. This could often be avoided if the final use of buildings was visualized at the design stage, allowing materials and finishes to be chosen which are capable of withstanding everyday wear and tear. In particular, it is sensible to avoid items that are imported or otherwise difficult to obtain locally.

The consequences
Whether the cause is inadequate finance, bad management, or poor building design, the consequences of poor maintenance are serious and potentially disastrous for the nation as a whole. Building maintenance has been defined as 'work undertaken in order to keep, restore, or improve every facility, that is every part of a building, its services and surrounds to a currently acceptable standard, and to sustain the utility and value of the

5

facility'.[1] Its functional role is therefore to retain the usefulness of the property, whether as a house or an office, within the acceptable standards of a 'reasonable user'. It is also concerned with maintaining the appearance of the property: first impressions are very important and the very reputation of the owner or occupants may be judged by appearance of external surfaces.

The financial role

The financial role of building maintenance is to preserve the physical condition of the capital asset: thus the level of maintenance should contain deterioration. Ideally, the optimum situation would be one whereby the marginal rates of substitution between maintenance and depreciation are equal, for example where a rise of one US dollar in maintenance leads to a fall of one dollar in depreciation. The rate of deterioration will therefore determine the level of maintenance expenditure over the life of the building. Unfortunately, under severe pressure for financial retrenchment in the face of rising expectations, many countries have been forced to cut maintenance budgets in recent years. For example, a report entitled *Growth, employment and equity: a comprehensive strategy for the Sudan*[2] referred to the apparently rapid deterioration of buildings and other structures due to inadequate regularity and standards of repair and maintenance. The report pointed out that:

'In the Sudan maintenance of public buildings is normally carried out by direct labour. Arrangements vary, but a fixed percentage of building costs is usually allocated on an annual basis for repairs and maintenance. Up to about 1965, the most common system was to allocate 1.5 per cent of total cost per year, and to carry out preventive maintenance every third year, using the accrued fund of about 4.5 per cent to repair and redecorate the building fully. Unfortunately, repair and maintenance budgets have been cut considerably in recent years, with the result that standards are falling drastically in public buildings. Short-term economies of this kind are rarely cost-effective in the longer term, and it is clear that numerous public buildings are deteriorating to the point where they cease to provide an efficient working environment and their useful lives are being shortened. In addition, repair and maintenance work has a high labour content and consequently makes only slight demands on the pool of available capital. By the adoption of

1. *Report of the Committee on Building Maintenance* (HMSO, London, 1972).
2. *Growth, employment and equity: a comprehensive strategy for the Sudan* (ILO, Geneva, 1976).

6

planned preventive maintenance with proper inspection and supervision, it would be possible to increase present levels of productivity and to provide useful additional employment opportunities.'

This was no isolated case, and there is a general need for more information to be gathered and analysed on the effects of reduced maintenance budgets on the value of national building stocks.

Lack of research

Very little theoretical or empirical research has been done on the subject of building maintenance in the context of developing countries. Moreover, the relationship between design and the subsequent costs of maintenance has been particularly neglected. In many countries so little attention is paid to the subject of building maintenance that it is commonplace for buildings to be pulled down and rebuilt well before the end of their potential economic lives. Indeed, it is mainly in those countries where conservation is an issue and conservationists are active that there has been an incentive to look again at the potential for rehabilitation. Although this pressure was initially based on aesthetic and other non-financial considerations, many clients have been pleasantly surprised to find that rehabilitation is actually a paying proposition.

To some extent the problem is a statistical one, since there are many countries where new buildings are 'counted' but rehabilitated ones are not. In such countries the official institutions tend to limit their activities to providing new facilities, so that the figures which are used to measure their achievements appear in the most favourable light. It is a curious commentary on the methods of public administration that activities which are counted as 'costs' are neglected until the statistical basis changes; then they suddenly become 'benefits'. If maintenance expenditure was accepted as a measure of the benefit to the owner and/or user in terms of financial return, efficiency, effectiveness or quality of life, the situation would be transformed. In other words, there is a case for suggesting that building maintenance will not be accorded the importance it deserves until presented in a different way.

In Kenya, for instance, it is very unusual to find any comprehensive maintenance records, whether in public or private organizations. The records on maintenance costs are generally kept for accounting purposes and are rarely used for maintenance research. In Ghana the situation appears to be worse; a 1982 study concluded that:

'Infrastructure and housing utilities have suffered general neglect. This situation has aroused a lot of concern. It has been noted that factors underlying the poor health status of the population are related to poor sanitary and housing conditions and poor water supplies amongst others. Neglect of daily and periodical maintenance has led to rapid deterioration in most of the older estates, especially the rental units. Tenants ignore their responsibility for internal repairs. But the developers are equally culpable of renegading on their external repairs. The high cost of repairs coupled with the low rental values seem to justify the neglect. The poor system of garbage collection by the local authorities accounts for the filth that has become part and parcel of the estate landscape.'[3]

Of particular relevance is the statement that the high cost of repairs combined with low rental values justifies the neglect of property maintenance. This would imply that buildings when let are not bringing a high enough return to finance adequate maintenance. This is a common problem for housing authorities, and they are faced with a real dilemma in setting rents low enough to be affordable but high enough to be economic. Ideally, tenants should be helped and encouraged to carry out routine maintenance and repairs, but if this process is not planned and managed, and backed up by some system of inspection and advice, the results will be haphazard, at best.

In Nigeria, Wahab reports that 'all available evidences suggest that, in general, buildings are not managed properly in Nigeria. Buildings are undermaintained for a variety of reasons, ranging from ignorance, wrong priorities, preference for new projects, the immorality of contracting in Nigeria which results in contract awards to incompetent contractors, undue favouritisms and erroneous feelings that whatever is maintained is invariably inferior to new buildings.'[4]

According to Mogbo, 'present clients and designers in Nigeria are often reluctant to recommend local materials because of lack of information on this aspect. Others support the patronizing of local materials because of their initial costs, but fail to consider maintenance, while after-sales service is often not available.'[5]

3. A.K. Amonoo, *Housing provision, the Ghana situation: exposition, critique and appraisal*, M.Sc. Project (University of Reading, 1982).
4. K.A. Wahab, 'Maintenance management and physical performance of buildings,' *The Tropical Environment* (Faculty of Environmental Studies, University of Nigeria, 1980).
5. T.M. Mogbo, 'Priority on planning stage: local materials in Nigerian construction,' *Chartered Surveyor* (1980).

This evidence from two African countries may or may not be typical. What is certain is that Kenya and Nigeria are two of the very few countries where *any* research on building maintenance has been undertaken. For most African countries, organized and analysed data which could define the size of the maintenance problem is simply not available. A case has to be made for decision-makers to take a comprehensive overview of building investment based upon cost and value over the many years of occupation rather than just the initial cost and appearance. In view of the current dearth of knowledge and experience, almost any hard data would be welcome. However, the most urgent need is for research in the following areas:

Influence of design on maintenance
Maintenance cost determinants
Organization and administration of building maintenance
Information systems for building maintenance
Service life of buildings.

A Cinderella activity
In many developing countries maintenance is regarded as 'Cinderella' activity to be performed on an *ad hoc* basis as the need arises. It is also seen as a function entirely separate from design and construction, when in fact it is an integral part of the process of creating and maintaining wealth. Under the circumstancë opportunities are lost for accumulating and analysing information which could then be fed back to designers and contractors in order to encourage good practice and, equally important, discourage the use of features and components that regularly give rise to maintenance problems.

The objective should be to determine which aspects of design and construction are causing maintenance problems, and to establish an optimum maintenance expenditure. It is thus necessary to carry out research by quantitative analysis rather than casual observation. It serves little purpose to note that buildings are poorly maintained without ascertaining whether they are economically maintainable. To consider the cost of maintenance implies that an acceptable maintenance standard will have to be agreed on, and only then can one judge whether buildings are well-maintained or otherwise.

A management problem
Even in the developed countries where some research is being carried out on the subject of maintenance, priority is given to the *technical* aspects of building maintenance, particularly the

9

durability of materials and the life-span of construction methods. General workshops and seminars do take place, but the papers presented are often laboratory studies carried out under accelerated conditions, with little attention directed to the cost of the materials used. In some countries with a high proportion of public housing, some work is being carried out on organizational aspects such as the involvement of tenants or residents in maintenance work, although little emphasis appears to be placed on financial management.

While developing countries are soliciting funds for the provision of low-cost housing projects, it is imperative that they should not lose sight of the questions of how the facilities would be maintained, and their economic life. Pioneering research in Kenya reveals, for instance, that some local authorities spend as much as 50 per cent of rental revenues on maintaining housing estates, with the result that there is no hope of building-up funds to replace housing when it becomes obsolete. No doubt this maintenance is urgently needed, but experience shows that if maintenance costs exceed 15 per cent of rental revenue there is little chance of raising funds to replace the houses in due course.

The main reasons for excessive maintenance costs are inappropriate design and construction together with poor maintenance management. In Kenya it appeared that design faults accounted for 14 per cent of the variation in maintenance costs, simply because of an inappropriate choice of building materials and poor design of facilities. A further revelation of poor maintenance management in Kenya is that, on average, nearly 42 per cent of maintenance jobs are never attended to after being reported. It is also known that nearly all the maintenance activity results from tenants' complaints rather than planned inspection. What are the reasons for this sad state of affairs? Maintenance managers are legendary sufferers from resource starvation. Money, materials and almost everything else (apart from complaints!) are directed towards new projects. In Kenya, maintenance managers gave four main reasons for their inability to carry out an efficient maintenance service in public buildings:[6]

	per cent
lack of materials	60
lack of staff/supervisors and operatives	24
lack of transport	5
other causes	11

6. P.M. Syagga, *Management of Local Authority Housing Estates in Kenya*, MA Thesis (University of Nairobi, 1979).

These are essentially management rather than technical problems, which arise because public institutions not only give low
priority to maintenance in their expenditure budgets, but, even
more seriously, they neglect the basic principles of organizing
maintenance so as to provide labour, materials and equipment
of the right kind and at the right time and place. Maintenance
managers for government buildings in Kenya have experienced
cuts in maintenance budgets in the order of 38.1 per cent since
1976, and are therefore well aware that finance, like any other
resource, is rarely adequate. This consideration makes the need
for sound management practices even more urgent.

A maintenance handbook
Setting up an adequate information system for building maintenance requires a systematic approach to data collection,
processing and communication so as to serve both the managers
concerned with the maintenance of existing stock and the
designers of new buildings. It is therefore necessary to examine
the needs of the people who will use the information, whether
they are sponsors, builders, designers or users, in order to
determine the sources, nature, and mode of presentation.

Given the diversity of the sources of information, the
maintenance department should accumulate a data bank of
management information on which to base decisions. The
information should be classified to allow for easy retrieval of the
documents: the systematic collection and dissemination of such
information is crucial. Maintenance departments should aim to
improve productivity by reducing maintenance costs, a move
which will warrant feedback on common defects with a range of
appropriate remedies. Such information will help in the preparation of a building maintenance handbook; a handbook which
should provide all building users with a common system of
maintenance information recording and retrieval for the guidance of maintenance operatives, building owners, occupiers,
and designers of future buildings.

The need for a maintenance handbook grows with the
increased complexity of buildings such as office blocks and
conference centres. Such structures demand specialist inspection and servicing due to the installation of sophisticated heating
and air conditioning systems; as well as lifts and other specialist
plant and equipment. A maintenance handbook could provide a
convenient form of communication between designers, owners,
maintenance managers and users. The handbook will be initi-
ated by the designer, then regularly updated by the maintenance

11

department to show all maintenance work carried out in each element, any changes, improvements or rehabilitation work, and all 'as-built' drawings, where changes are made from initial drawings.

Typical contents

A typical building maintenance handbook for each property should include the following points:

1. A brief history of the property, including names and addresses of consultants and contractors.
2. A short specification outlining constructional processes, components, principal materials and finishes. All hidden features should be described and special features noted, including methods of fixing, repair or replacement, dismantling and reconstruction.
3. 'As-built' plans with sections and elevations wherever possible.
4. Information on housekeeping and routine maintenance with details of both internal and external surfaces and decorations, including schedules for cleaning, inspection and maintenance.
5. Information on the means of operating mechanical, electrical and plumbing installations, with details of requisite maintenance or servicing.
6. Descriptions of renovations, extensions, adaptations and repairs to each element.

The handbook should contain job descriptions for the tradesmen hired to carry out the maintenance tasks. It should also establish a link between the designer, the client, the managers and the users, who should be encouraged to work together as a team for the design and construction of new buildings.

Public participation

There is a growing awareness that human society depends primarily on personal responsibility rather than public control for the full and proper use of resources. Turner has argued that the management and maintenance of dwellings and their surroundings, and therefore their longevity, depend primarily on their residents and users.[7] Consequently, it is suggested that large organizations should have little or no business building or managing dwellings, rather that they should simply provide the infrastructure, as well as the tools and materials that people can use to maintain the buildings that they occupy.

7. J.F.C. Turner, *Housing By People: Towards Autonomy in Building Environments* (New York, 1976).

Turner also makes a point, reinforced by reports, that the construction and management costs of publicly sponsored low-cost housing schemes are often at least twice those of equivalent housing built by the informal sector. But ownership is not the sole factor; one can also point to inefficient construction management practices resulting in higher costs and extra time. Premature deterioration and vandalism are also rampant in publicly-provided rental housing, while privately owned accommodation is often better maintained. Here again it is not just a question of ownership, but also of management efficiency between the private houseowner and a centrally-controlled public authority. The procedures in a public authority are frequently cumbersome, whether for a new construction or maintenance works. There is thus a need for a flexible approach to the management of public organizations dealing with building maintenance, rather than the corporate approach that so often slows down decision-making processes.

Whatever one's attitude to new construction, there is already a large stock of publicly-provided housing in developing countries that must be maintained to provide shelter for those who cannot provide it for themselves. Experiments have been tried in countries such as the United Kingdom and Sweden[8] allowing tenants to carry out some maintenance within their premises. The tenant has a right to tackle certain simple improvements within the dwelling without obtaining the landlord's agreement: this applies mainly to painting and other tasks which do not demand advanced craft skills, and could not adversely affect the structural integrity of the building or the safety of the occupants. In some cases, tenants' committees have been formed to carry out repairs within given estates. Although the experiments have been interesting, the arrangements have not been notably successful. The committees have been characterized by low attendance at formal meetings, while the authority is faced with the difficulty of deciding which type of maintenance it should assign to tenants. Some maintenance tasks are extensive and thus costly, requiring a great deal of work. Also, the skills of the tenants may not be good enough to undertake the task.

Advocates of public participation in maintenance must take account of the practical difficulties. Of course, there are real benefits to be gained from the participation of occupants in building maintenance decisions. Residents are experts in their

8. Hijarne, 'Tenant Influence upon Housing Management,' *Research on Maintenance and Modernization* (CIB Proceedings, Rotterdam, 1979).

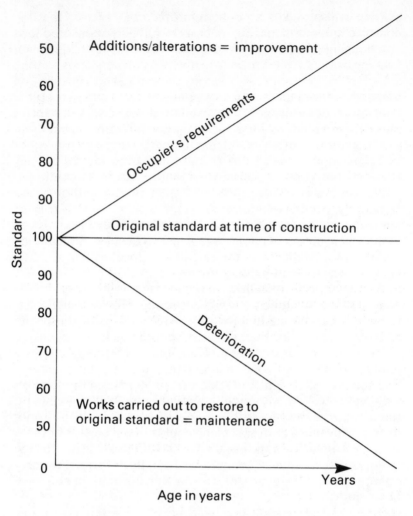

Figure 1.1 *Relationship between improvement and maintenance needs.*

own environments; they can give priority to measures marked out for their neighbourhood and have a greater control over the state of the area. But their requirements may differ from those of the owner as shown in Figure 1.1 In many cases, tenants' aspirations may be higher than is called for to support existing investments, in which case the work may be sanctioned by the owner but not subsidized from property maintenance funds. Thus what they regard as maintenance may in fact be improvements, with standards raised beyond those intended when the

14

building was designed. Adding a bathroom to a house or replacing louvered windows with glazed steel casements is an improvement: the definition of maintenance *vis-à-vis* improvements must therefore be carefully spelt out in the handbook.

Policy statement

If an authority decides to encourage public participation in housing maintenance, a first step is to prepare a statement of maintenance policy and procedures which clearly spells out the respective roles of building owners and the participating public, and describes how each group will be funded. It will also be necessary to state clearly the minimum level of maintenance regarded as acceptable by the authority, and to outline inspection procedures to ensure compliance. Any incentives such as material subsidies or rent 'holidays' to compensate for tenants' maintenance efforts should be recorded, together with charges made for work carried out by the authority if its tenant fails to meet the required standards. It may also be helpful to provide training to tenants through practical demonstrations on a model house, to help those who are motivated but lack the necessary skills.

Complexity

This chapter will have achieved something if it has established the complexity of the subject of building maintenance. In essence, it is concerned with the use of resources available to protect buildings, as capital assets, from decay, and to ensure that they provide satisfactory shelter for the people who live and work in them. Thus, if the subject is complex, the benefits can be simply stated. If these benefits are to be achieved, it is essential that maintenance is accorded the priority that it deserves in national development programmes of developing countries.

The next stage is to establish a clear policy to ensure that capital assets are maintained in good structural safety both for the users and the owners. Preferably, the policy should go further, aiming to ensure satisfactory living or working conditions for the occupants based on agreed standards. In many developing countries today, existing regulations that stipulate standards of maintenance are vague and haphazard, and do not have the force of law to ensure that they are complied with.

As suggested earlier, it would be beneficial if all buildings were provided with handbooks before certificates of occupation are issued. Owners could use them as a base from which to establish standardized maintenance procedures covering regular inspections and target expenditure. A system of monitoring should be established on the state of buildings and the maintenance work carried out, whether by the private or public sector, so that governments will be in a position to judge whether the policy is appropriate and effective.

CHAPTER 2

The Economics of Building Maintenance

Maintenance function

The function of maintenance can be divided into three groups: cleaning and servicing, rectification and repair, and replacement. Timely expenditure on the first two can postpone the need to replace materials or components, a very expensive business. Cleaning and servicing should be carried out regularly and may be combined with a system of reporting faults, so that repairs can be carried out soon after faults become apparent, thereby avoiding the need for more expensive repairs or even replacement at a later stage.

The cleaning and servicing operation is usually the responsibility of the building occupier. It can be described as day to day maintenance, and is normally a labour-intensive operation carried out by the occupier of a house or, in an office or commercial building, by part-time employees. The frequency of each cleaning job depends on the type of operation: for example, floors are usually swept daily, but polished weekly; windows can be cleaned monthly and decoration will only take place every few years. Other important maintenance tasks which should be carried out regularly but are frequently neglected include cleaning out gutters and checking drains.

Unfortunately the maintenance function is often seen as entirely separate from the construction process although, in reality, it is an integral part. This has had the unfortunate effect of encouraging designers to ignore the cost of maintaining the structures for which they are responsible.

Sophisticated property owners now appreciate that the commissioning of new buildings should be based on the 'total cost in use', rather than the 'purchase cost'. A parallel may be drawn with the purchase of a motor vehicle, where the intelligent buyer estimates the likely cost of repairs, servicing and depreciation, as well as comparing retail prices.

Maintenance economics

The economics of building maintenance represents an attempt to determine the use of resources available for maintenance so as to maintain the structural safety of buildings and provide a reasonable return on capital assets, while providing an acceptable living or working environment for the occupants. It is a fact that in developing as well as developed countries, many building owners, whether in commerce and industry or residential estates, are unaware of the cost of maintaining their properties and do not have a means of predicting how much they ought to be spending to keep their buildings at an effective standard.

The point has already been made that buildings should be appraised at the design stage or at the time of purchase so as to determine both the initial and long-term maintenance costs. Maintenance should not be seen as an add-on luxury, but recognized as part of the process of creating new assets and resource allocation in the construction activity. A competent manager should be in a position to state where, when and how much should be spent on maintenance. Appraisal techniques such as cost-in-use, discounted cash flow and cost-benefit analysis can assist in determining the answers to these questions. All such techniques are concerned with comparing different means to the same end, and not with defining the end itself. That is, they help in the choice of means to a given end, and with the problem of obtaining the best value for money for the resources spent. The ends, such as user requirements for comfort and the level of running and maintenance costs, have to be conceptually determined, preferably at the time of acquiring the property. This leads to an examination of the criteria that exist to determine the balance between acquisition costs and future maintenance costs.

Initial and running costs
It is often suggested that an inverse relationship exists between initial costs and the costs of the user. Initial costs refer either to the cost of purchasing a property or the cost of developing a new building. Running costs include cleaning, rectification and repair, and replacement, but may also take in the recurrent costs of heating, lighting and other services. In principle, a reduction in future maintenance costs may be obtained by increasing initial costs; similarly economies in initial costs may be gained from the acceptance of an increased level of maintenance costs.

The preferences for low or high initial costs will depend on time preferences and commercial judgement; so that speculative developers who build for sale on immediate completion will generally give greater regard to economies in initial costs than in user costs. Purchasers, on the other hand, will show

18

greater concern for the latter. Public housing estates such as those of a local authority are developed as a long-term asset, and the housing authority will seek to strike a balance that provides reasonably low initial costs as well as low maintenance costs.

One good reason for accepting high initial costs is that cheaper materials often (but not always) require more frequent maintenance and may have a shorter working life than more expensive alternatives. This assumption is based on examples of wall finishes, floor surfaces, moving parts of machinery and ironmongery. While some of the examples given may be valid, expensive specifications do not always buy long-term economies. Plastered and painted walls are expensive in both initial and maintenance costs when compared to rough-cast rendering, as are wood-block floors in relation to simple floor screeds. (It is ironic that in buildings of prestige most floors are carpeted irrespective of whether expensively finished in parquet or wood-blocks, or cheaply in screeds). The choice of building materials is not the only factor affecting initial costs of construction or maintenance.

Strategic design
Site conditions and labour costs are other variables. Labour, for instance, may account for as much as 45 per cent of the development cost of certain low-cost housing schemes in developing countries, despite a high proportion of semi-skilled labour of 85 per cent and only 15 per cent skilled labour. Besides, the cost of a building is not necessarily a measure of its quality, both technically and functionally. A lavish building may also be expensive to maintain. Poorly designed and constructed buildings may cost as much or more than a well-designed and properly-constructed building, depending on management and productivity at the construction site. Thus what is important in reducing future maintenance costs is the strategic design of the building; that is its shape, orientation, wall or floor ratio, and so on rather than high initial costs. Perhaps high initial costs *would* be appropriate where a high standard of construction and finish is required irrespective of the economic considerations.

The low-cost housing dilemma
In developing countries a respectable case may be made for requiring low initial costs, particularly in housing projects, so as to provide maximum accommodation with the available funds. This explains the proliferation of low-cost housing schemes on site and service projects which are inevitably storing up trouble

19

for the future, as income is bound to be insufficient to fund proper maintenance. The result is rampant and premature decay through lack of maintenance.

It is thought socially unacceptable to choose higher initial costs, as this would reduce the number of the accommodation units to be provided with available funds. This proposition is at the root of the low-cost housing dilemma. Excessive maintenance costs soon eat into future revenue from rentals thereby limiting the provision of more housing; thus housing development ceases to be replicable. Some local authorities have to spend as much as 50 per cent of their rental revenue on maintenance and repairs. They are caught in a vicious circle: because they are running low-cost housing estates rents have to be kept low, and because rents are low, maintenance is poor.

Budget constraints

While it is true that many existing buildings could have better maintenance characteristics than they currently exhibit, evidence suggests that minimizing maintenance liability is a matter of careful initial design and selection of components and materials rather than a function of capital cost. If budget constraints have to be considered, however, then their effects on the long-term maintenance of the buildings must be considered. It should be possible to estimate the annual maintenance costs of a proposed design. On the assumption that the purpose of maintenance is to preserve the structure of the building during its economic life, it is reasonable to assume that the total expenditure on maintenance (discounted) should be added to the initial capital expenditure (less scrap value discounted from the time of the demise of the building), so that:

Cost in use $= C + M - S$
where $C =$ the initial capital cost
        $M =$ the sum of discounted values of annual maintenance
        $S =$ the scrap value of the building (discounted)

Assuming that the scrap value is nil when the building ceases to perform its function, the cost-in-use will be equal to the capital cost plus the sum of discounted maintenance costs.

Figure 2.1 illustrates the effects of decisions on costs taken at various stages of the life cycle of a typical building. Although the discounted future running costs of this building are as great as the initial development costs, the pattern of maintenance needs is set much earlier in the decision-making process. This means that the magnitude of maintenance costs has to be anticipated

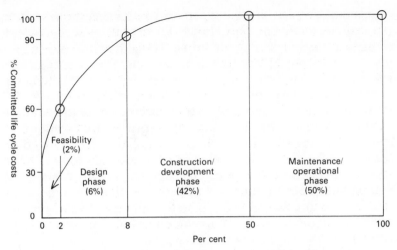

Figure 2.1 *Effects of early decisions on building life-cycle costs.*

during the design phase. While feasibility and design amount to only some eight per cent of the total project cost, the decisions made during this time commit nearly 95 per cent of the cost of the building's total life. This shows that costs during both the construction and maintenance phases are very largely dependent on the initial decisions and parameters agreed between the client and the designer, emphasizing the significance of design in determining future maintenance costs.

Discounting and capitalization

The costs attributable to a building occur at different times in its life, the pattern varying with the design features. These costs must be judged on a common basis before comparisons can be made: either they can be discounted and compared in terms of present values, or their annual equivalents can be used as a basis of comparison.

To obtain the sum of maintenance costs for a particular building a process called *discounting* is used. Future maintenance costs are estimated year by year, discounted, brought to present value, then added up. The technique can be used whether annual maintenance costs are estimated to vary from year to year or are expected to be approximately constant, although the latter calculation is less cumbersome.

Discounting calculations

The basic principle upon which discount calculations rest is quite simple. A dollar spent a year from today is less of a burden

21

than a dollar which has to be spent today. If interest rates of ten per cent are available, only about 91 cents will be needed today to have a full dollar in a year's time. If the debt falls due in two years, then some 82.5 cents will be enough. The same principle can be applied to future income, as a dollar of income today is worth more than the promise of a dollar next year. Fortunately, there are formulae and tables to ease these calculations.

Mathematicians have worked out a formula which allows us to calculate the present worth of one dollar to be received or spent. It gives the present value (PV) of the right to receive or spend one dollar at the end of each year for 'n' years at 'i' compound interest (expressed in decimals, that is, ten per cent interest is expressed as 0.10). The formula is derived from the addition of the present values of one dollar for each dollar received or spent. It follows that:

$$\text{PV of \$1 after one year} = \frac{1}{1+i}$$

$$\text{PV of \$1 after two years} = \frac{1}{(1+i)^2}$$

So, if the same annual maintenance expenditure goes on for a total period of n years, the present value of the total expenditure will be given by the series:

$$\text{PV of \$1 for n years} =$$
$$\frac{1}{(1+i)} + \frac{1}{(1+i)^2} + \ldots + \frac{1}{(1+i)^{n-1}} + \frac{1}{(1+i)^n}$$

Fortunately, there is no need to add up each item in the series every time this calculation is made (n years for a typical building can be quite a long time)! In order to simplify the formula, a rather elegant transformation is used. The trick is to multiply both sides of the equation by $(1+i)$ to produce:

$$(1+i) \times PV = 1 + \frac{1}{(1+i)} + \frac{1}{(1+i)^2} + \quad + \frac{1}{(1+i)^{n-1}}$$

It is immediately obvious that all but the last item in the first series and the first item (number 1) in the second series are exactly the same. So, by subtracting the first equation from the second, the whole formula is simplified to:

$$i \times PV = 1 - \frac{1}{(1+i)^n}$$

By dividing both sides of the equation by the compound interest rate i, a relatively simple formula is reached:

$$PV = \dfrac{1 - \dfrac{1}{(1+i)^n}}{i}$$

Fortunately even this formula does not have to be worked out bn every occasion, since tables are available from which the same information can be obtained more conveniently. Table 2.1

Table 2.1 Present value calculation – fixed annual cost assumed interest rate: ten per cent

Year	Cost	Discount factor	Present value
1	200	0.909	181
2	200	0.826	165
3	200	0.751	150
4	200	0.682	136
5	200	0.621	124
6	200	0.564	112
7	200	0.513	112
8	200	0.466	93
9	200	0.424	85
10	200	0.386	77
		Total	$1,225

Table 2.2 Present value calculation – varying annual cost assumed interest rate: ten per cent

Year	Cost	Discount factor	Present value
1	100	0.909	91
2	300	0.826	248
3	600	0.751	450
4	1,000	0.682	682
5	1,000	0.621	621
6	1,000	0.564	564
7	1,000	0.513	513
8	1,000	0.466	466
9	1,000	0.424	424
10	1,000	0.386	386
		Total	$4,445

illustrates the present value of a recurring annual cost of $200 over a period of ten years at a ten per cent rate of interest. But costs do not always remain the same year after year. A new building (like a new car) needs less maintenance in its early years. This, too, can be allowed for in present value calculations, as illustrated in Table 2.2.

If the discounting technique described above is applied to a building with an initial cost of 1,000 units, but maintained at an annual cost of 100 units over a period of 20 years, the present value of expenditure at ten per cent is given by:

$$V = A \left\{ \frac{1 - \left(\frac{1}{(1+i)^n} \right)}{i} \right\}$$

where V = present worth of future expenditure
A = regular fixed expenditure per year
n = number of years over which expenditure is incurred
i = interest percentage at which sums spent accumulate

$$\textit{so that} \quad V = 100 \left\{ \frac{1 - \left(\frac{1}{(1.1)^{20}} \right)}{0.1} \right\} = 100 \times 8.5136$$

Therefore, the present value V of $100 per annum = $851.36. On the basis of this calculation, the PV of the maintenance costs of $100 per annum is slightly lower than the initial cost of $1,000. If the total running costs were taken into account including insurance and property taxes, the two figures would be comparable. In fact, the present value of the stream of maintenance expenditure required to keep a building in a satisfactory condition is often equal to or greater than the initial cost, so that trade-offs between the two are well worth considering.

The method of calculating the present value of discounted maintenance costs is not without its drawbacks. The use of high discount rates renders the present worth of reducible maintenance costs small in relation to capital costs, unless realistic provision is made for future cost increases. The PV of maintenance and repair costs can appear negligible if the estimated building life exceeds 20 years. Table 2.3 serves to illustrate the effects of interest rates and discounting periods on the PVs of periodic maintenance expenditures, of, say $100.

24

Table 2.3 PVs in $ for varying periods at various rates

Discount rate (%)	PV of $100 at end of period in years						
	10	20	30	40	50	60	100
5	61.4	37.7	23.1	14.2	8.7	5.3	0.7
10	38.6	14.8	5.7	2.2	0.8	0.3	0.0
15	24.7	6.1	1.5	0.4	0.0	0.0	0.0
20	16.1	2.6	0.4	0.0	0.0	0.0	0.0
25	10.7	1.1	0.1	0.0	0.0	0.0	0.0

The PVs become progressively smaller as the interest rates increase, so that even at 15 per cent, the PV at 30 years is negligible. After 40 years, the discounting factor becomes relatively stable, so that it does not matter whether a maintenance cost is incurred at the 50th year or the 100th year. Thus, the estimation of a building's life and when maintenance costs will be incurred is a sensitive issue, as is the choice of an appropriate discount rate.

Annual equivalent
An alternative to showing the relative magnitude of discounted maintenance costs to initial costs is to compare annual equivalents of the initial capital and running costs. That is, using an appropriate mortgage lending rate, of say 15 per cent, it is possible to calculate how much needs to be repaid every year to redeem the capital over the estimated life of the building. The amount of repayment, called annuity, is then compared with the estimated annual maintenance cost. This is a measure of how much would be saved in future expenditure for every extra dollar spent initially. Where the two figures are equal is the break even point, given the building life and interest rate. The break even ratios decline with the life of the building, so that the shorter the life the less it is worth spending to reduce maintenance costs. So, the shorter the life the greater the maintenance costs relative to initial costs which it is worthwhile to bear. Increases in interest rates have the same sort of effect as a reduction in the building's life, so that the higher the rate of interest, the greater the need to save in expenditure for each dollar in initial costs. The shorter the life and the higher the rate of interest, the more worthwhile it is to limit the initial costs and to postpone expenditure to the future.

The annual equivalent calculation also uses discounting techniques to calculate the annuity or sinking fund payments that are required over a given number of years at various rates of interest for each dollar of capital outlay. The formula needed to calculate this is based on an old friend:

$$V = A \left\{ \frac{1 - \left(\frac{1}{(1+i)^n}\right)}{i} \right\}$$

In this case, P (the development cost) will be substituted for V (the present worth of future expenditure), and E (the annuity of equal annual payments) for A (the regular fixed expenditure per year):

$$P = E \left\{ \frac{1 - \left(\frac{1}{(1+i)^n}\right)}{i} \right\}$$

It is E that must be calculated this time, so the formula must be manipulated a little, first by multiplying both sides of the equation by i and dividing by E, so:

$$\frac{P \times i}{E} = 1 - \frac{1}{(1+i)^n}$$

Then the right-hand side of the equation is simplified to:

$$\frac{P \times i}{E} = \frac{(1+i)^n - 1}{(1+i)^n}$$

Next, both sides of the equation are reversed to give:

$$\frac{E}{P \times i} = \frac{(1+i)^n}{(1+i)^n - 1}$$

All that remains is to multiply both sides of the equation by P × i to produce the following formula to calculate E:

$$E = P \left\{ \frac{i(1+i)^n}{(1+i)^n - 1} \right\}$$

where E = the annuity or equal annual repayments
         P = the initial development cost
         i = rate of interest per annum
         n = term of years of building life

For instance, the annual equivalent of $1,000 of development cost over 20 years at a ten per cent interest rate would be given by:

$$E = 1,000 \times \left\{ \frac{0.1(1.1)^{20}}{(1.1)^{20}-1} \right\} = 1000 \times 0.1175$$

Therefore, the annual equivalent of $1,000 = $117.5

If the annual maintenance cost is $100, then, as seen in the previous example, the annual maintenance cost is close to the annual equivalent of the initial cost and possible trade-offs between the two are worth examining.

Cost in use
While the two alternative discounting methods presented above could be used to relate maintenance costs to initial costs, allowing a decision on an appropriate design in cost terms, in practice designers also have to consider the relative total cost-in-use of design alternatives. The choice will usually fall on the least total-cost solution. That is, for each design alternative, initial cost is added to discounted running costs, so that as discounting factors recede with interest rates and longer lives, initial costs become more pronounced as the design determinant. Only shorter lives and lower interest rates give maintenance real prominence as a determining factor. This could be misleading, particularly in countries with a pronounced inflationary trend in the cost of building materials and the wages of the skilled craftsmen required for specialized maintenance tasks.

Design alternatives: an example
A developer is presented with two alternative building designs:

	Building A	Building B
Initial cost ($)	65,000	50,000
Annual maintenance cost ($)	500	1,000
Life of building	60 years	40 years

With a discount rate of ten per cent, which proposal should be adopted? The alternatives will be compared on the basis of cost-in-use which takes into account both initial costs. The cost-in-use can vary widely according to specification of the building and the way it is used, but it is usually possible to estimate such costs from data for similar buildings.

In terms of cost-in-use, building B is apparently cheaper than building A, even though building B costs more to maintain. However, there are other factors to consider. Building B will

27

Table 2.4 Cost-in-use calculation

	Building A	Building B
Initial cost ($)	65,000	50,000
Present value of maintenance cost ($)	500 for 60 years at 10 per cent, i.e. 500×9.97 = 4,985	1,000 for 40 years at 10 per cent, i.e. 1000×9.78 = 9,780
Therefore cost-in-use ($)	= 69,985	59,780

presumably have to be replaced after 40 years, whereas building A will have another 20 years of economic life ahead of it. Much will depend upon how far ahead the developer wishes to look.

If the 40-year period is used as a basis for comparison, the discount factor for building A should be reduced to 9.78. But in this case the choice will still fall on building B, unless a realistic allowance is made for the value of building A 40 years from now and this is discounted back to present value. Alternatively, a 60-year comparison could be made, but this would necessitate an estimate of the cost of replacing building B after 40 years (with its own train of 20 years discounted maintenance expenditure), although this would be offset by an allowance for its future useful life at the end of the comparison period. (The authors appreciate that these alternative assumptions may be somewhat confusing, but are seeking to emphasize that the results of discounting should *not* be accepted uncritically and assumptions on economic life and on discount rates are very much open to challenge).

In terms of annual equivalents the calculation would be as follows:

Table 2.5 Annual equivalent calculation

	Building A		Building B	
Annual maintenance ($)		= 500		= 1,000
Annual annuity charge ($)	65,000	= 6,520	50,000	= 5,112
based on initial cost ($)	9.97		9.78	
Therefore annual equivalent ($)		= 7,020		= 6,112

The results again suggest that building B offers the cheaper solution even with its shorter life, but the same considerations apply as to the cost-in-use calculation. Either a 40-year or a 60-

28

year comparison period must be chosen, and a realistic allowance must be made for the value of whichever building (A or B/2 respectively) has not reached the end of its useful life.

Coping with uncertainty

Bearing in mind the various drawbacks and imponderables implicit in the above calculations, the reader may doubt that there is any place for analysis. Besides the choice of interest rates and the building's life, the estimation of future expenditure is fraught with uncertainty. Maintenance cost estimates are frequently based on operations that can be programmed, such as redecoration, replacement and possibly cleaning. This ignores much of what is called contingency maintenance which is not programmable. Recent research in Kenya, for instance, indicates that over 50 per cent of actual annual maintenance costs come into this category. A possible explanation for the common practice of overlooking contingency maintenance is the uncertainty of causal factors, such as intensity of use and changing maintenance requirements. The effectiveness of maintenance should also be considered in relation to its effect on rental income and building value. In this way, maintenance costs need to be optimized not only at the design stage, but also during the management of the building in use.

Nevertheless, and despite its undoubted drawbacks, analysis is preferable to guesswork. The assumptions – and the outcomes – should certainly be subjected to critical appraisal, but analysis does at least encourage the client and the designer to consider cost-in-use as well as initial costs. The frequent alternative of focusing on the latter to the exclusion of maintenance implications is both wasteful and unprofessional.

Choice

Although calculation plays an important part in the process of choice, it must be tempered with judgement and an appreciation of the importance of various factors which cannot necessarily be quantified, such as the appearance of the building and the personal preferences of the building's owner and future occupants. The role of calculation is to guide the process of choice, and the designer should be aware of all the variables that are available in order to reach an optimum solution. For example, it may be possible to substitute less expensive local materials. Technology is itself a variable. So, a simple but elegant design may be both cheap to build and to maintain using local contractors and local craftsmen, while it could also meet the client's needs as effectively as a more sophisticated alternative.

Maintenance cost levels

Most large industrial organizations have maintenance departments to ensure that machines, buildings, services and equipment achieve a predetermined level of productive efficiency and are available when required. Similar arrangements exist among organizations owning commercial buildings and housing accommodation. The need for maintenance is therefore accepted in general terms. However, there does not appear to be any agreed way of determining how much to spend on it.

In industry, inadequate plant maintenance would not only lead to costly repairs but also to lost production. The effect can be measured in terms of lost revenue, so the level of profitability provides a measure to determine how much maintenance needs to be done. If loss of production arises directly out of plant breakdowns due to insufficient maintenance, then the cost of standby equipment, replacement units or extra maintenance can be calculated, and profitabilities compared. Equipment availability, then, may determine how much maintenance is necessary and what to spend on it.

Income comparison

The effect of poor maintenance is appreciated by companies which specialize in the development of commercial property. Poorly maintained properties command lower rents, are harder to let, and have shorter economic lives. Poor building maintenance, for instance, may shorten the life of a building from 60 to 40 years, while if a building is totally neglected it may only last 20 years. The following example (Figure 2.2) illustrates how inadequate maintenance can lead to deterioration and loss of value.

Effects of maintenance on a building's life: an example

The example is based on three similar buildings:

Building A, which is totally neglected, lasts 20 years
Building B, which is poorly maintained, lasts 40 years
Building C, which is well-maintained, lasts 60 years

All the buildings start with a rental of $1,000 per year, but there is a maintenance deduction of $100 per annum (ten per cent of income) for building B and $200 per annum (20 per cent of income) for building C. Reflecting the different levels of maintenance, annual rental increases of one, three and five per

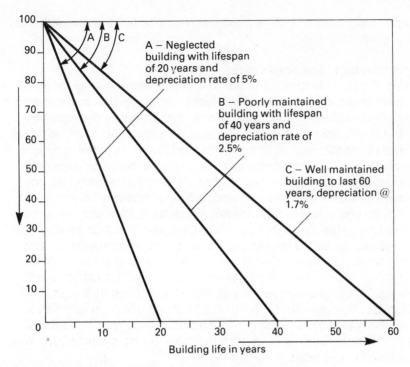

Figure 2.2 *Effect of maintenance on building life.*

cent respectively can be anticipated for buildings A, B and C. The outcome in terms of total income receivable is shown in Table 2.6

The differences in income receivable in the three cases above are dramatic, although the stream of income should itself be discounted back to present value to obtain a rigorous comparison. Nevertheless, there can be no doubt that commercial

Table 2.6 Comparison of PV of income receivable

	Building A	Building B	Building C
Income receivable in year I ($)	1,000	900	800
Annual increase (%)	1	3	5
Building life (n) (years)	20	40	60
Total income receivable in n years $(1+i)^n$ ($)	22,019	67,861	282,867
Ratio	1 :	3 :	13

31

property companies appreciate that good maintenance is a paying proposition.

Problems in the public sector

Of course it is more difficult for maintenance managers in the public sector to make out a case for adequate maintenance budgets. Even if notional rents are charged to the occupiers, these are rarely subject to commercial negotiation and the maintenance budget may be funded from a separate source. There is also a reluctance to revalue property either upwards or downwards, so the effect of good or bad maintenance on both capital values and potential income are effectively hidden. Even so, it should not be difficult to demonstrate that poor maintenance is a sign of poor stewardship, while effective maintenance represents an intelligent and worthwhile investment of public funds.

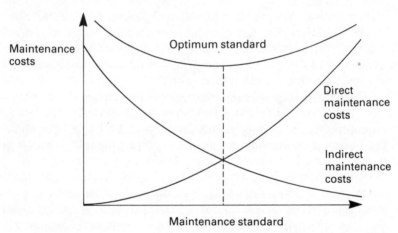

Figure 2.3 *Maintenance costs and standards (Source: Lee 1981)*

Direct and indirect costs

Figure 2.3 illustrates the relationship between maintenance standards and maintenance costs. It also separates direct from indirect costs, and shows the optimum standard of maintenance as the point where the total cost is at a minimum. Rising maintenance standards imply rising direct costs of maintenance while indirect costs fall with good maintenance. In Figure 2.3 direct costs refer to costs incurred in both preventive and corrective maintenance, that is, costs directly incurred in maintaining the facility. Indirect costs arise from inadequate repairs or servicing such as loss of production when a machine breaks down, or loss of income when a commercial building is poorly maintained. Indirect costs usually increase with frequent breakdowns arising from inadequate maintenance procedures. These costs will reduce if direct maintenance is better organized. There will therefore be a point where the sum of the two costs is at a minimum, and that becomes the optimal point of both expenditure and standard of maintenance.

Although the above model may not provide absolute measures of maintenance cost requirements, it at least gives some indication of an objective approach whereby both direct and indirect cost of repairs or servicing are considered to determine the standard of maintenance.

This formula assumes that maintenance cost is related to the replacement cost value of the asset. This may not be valid in cases of undermaintenance or overmaintenance, so that a mismatch exists between maintenance costs and the rate of deterioration. Where maintenance sufficiently arrests deterioration, a relationship can be established with a replacement cost value. But the formula is more of a comparative measure of efficiency of the maintenance programme rather than an absolute measure for maintenance costs.

The above theoretical optimization principles are generally relevant to commercial and industrial buildings where the aim of maintenance is to obtain maximum benefit from equipment. In building maintenance, however, maintenance cannot be tailored strictly to productivity. Good housekeeping may require more than is commercially optimal in terms of maintenance costs. Factors affecting comfort, safety and efficiency of employees such as cleanliness, tidiness, lighting, ventilation, heat, cold, noise, vibration, colour, adequate space, rest facilities, and elimination of fire hazards, may not affect machine availability, and therefore could be subordinated in terms of maintenance cost priorities. These factors affect design considerations as much as they affect decisions on optimal maintenance costs.

Profit maximization

If the concept of profit maximization is applied to residential buildings, maintenance is required to retain the value of the building so that it continues to provide user efficiency, and thus commands rent that maximizes return. Insufficient maintenance may lead to a progressive loss in value or decrease in user efficiency. Some mathematical models have been developed to determine the level of maintenance expenditure both under rent controls and the non-controlled rental market. These models suggest that the optimal maintenance rate is that which equates marginal value added due to good maintenance with the marginal cost of realizing the requisite maintenance standard. This is because at the time of sale, disposal or purchase, the marginal value of a quality increase in a building unit must equal the marginal sales value of that increase. The marginal value of maintenance is represented by the present value of the stream of future net earnings, that is, revenue minus costs. The net earnings figure can be reached by using the simple formula '$R = rg - pm - c(rm)$' where the net return R equals gross rent (rg) minus the market cost of maintenance inputs (pm) and adjustment costs c(rm).

Adjustment costs include foregone rents since the enjoyment of housing services is disrupted by maintenance activities, similar to indirect costs in the commercial and industrial buildings. For maximum open market profit, the optimal maintenance strategy equates the marginal value added due to maintenance to the marginal cost of maintenance including adjustment costs. Paradoxically, both rent control and strict building codes can adversely affect the rate of housing deterioration in the private sector. Very strict code enforcement may force landlords to abandon marginal property, since additional expenditure does not necessarily command higher rents. Similarly, under rent control, demand for the limited stock of available property is boosted and landlords tend to reduce maintenance expenditure accordingly.

Public buildings

In the private sector the level of maintenance expenditure is determined by the desire to maximize returns on a stream of property services. The returns can be measured in terms of occupancy and rental levels, which depend on the quality of services offered throughout the ownership of the building. The quality of services is a function of the soundness of the physical structure, user facilities and aesthetic appearance, all of which have to be retained over time by adequate maintenance.

Profit maximization is not the sole motive in building development, particularly in public institutions. Levels of maintenance may therefore be related to amenity maximization rather than profit. It is also worth noting that not every aspect of building deterioration is capable of being improved by maintenance, as other factors can intervene such as obsolescence or neighbour-

34

hood deterioration. So, the philosophy of pegging the level of maintenance expenditures to rental value may not be appropriate in all circumstances, particularly in rent-controlled properties, co-operative housing, service tenancies, or public institutions that earn no rent.

The concept of obsolescence

Depreciation is an economic effect caused by either physical deterioration, functional obsolescence, economic obsolescence or a combination of any two or all three. It has been suggested that physical deterioration or depreciation accounts for only a minor part of total depreciation, and that most properties suffer their greatest loss in value from the effects of obsolescence.

In its broadest sense obsolescence is a loss in value for reasons other than physical deterioration. The test of obsolescence is whether or not local demand is sufficiently strong to warrant the cost of reconstruction of a property if it were to be destroyed and then rebuilt with the same design and quality of construction. If market conditions do not warrant such rebuilding, the property is subject to some form of value-reducing obsolescence.

This suggests that reconstruction or maintenance may not by themselves improve the demand for services of a building that suffers from obsolescence. Such actions would merely restore the physical depreciation of a structure that has ceased to be appropriate for its purpose. Value-reducing obsolescence may be functional or economic.

Functional obsolescence

Functional obsolescence is the loss in value arising from decreased utility, inadequacy, incapacity, or changes in architectural style which are inherent in the structure itself. The building may be an overimprovement or an underimprovement; the equipment may be obsolete; the rooms too small; the ceilings too high; the light inadequate or else the architectural plan, style and design may be poor. Thus all these characteristics that effectively diminish the value of a property may be classified as functional obsolescence.

It is evident that functional obsolescence arises from errors or omissions in a design that failed to anticipate changes in user requirement, and an inappropriate building may have to be improved rather than merely maintained. In many cases, costs incurred in undertaking property improvements may be regarded as capital expenditure rather than charges against revenue. Where profit maximization is the motivating factor,

35

however, such costs have to be amortized and added to annual maintenance costs. In other words improvements, like maintenance, have to pay their way. A well-designed improvement can reduce subsequent maintenance costs, since unsuitably designed buildings create a need for maintenance. An example is the intensive use of rooms or facilities that are inadequate, while dissatisfaction by users often leads to wanton damage, neglect or vandalism.

Economic obsolescence

Economic obsolescence is a loss in value resulting from conditions outside the building, which adversely affect its character and degree of use. It may arise from demographic factors such as population movements, income levels and consumption habits or local nuisances and hazards, a lack of community facilities or adverse legislation.

Like functional obsolescence, economic obsolescence has the effect of reducing demand for properties in the area concerned. The reduced demand is reflected in lower rent in comparison with similar properties in more desirable neighbourhoods. Where the motive for maintenance is profit maximization, economic obsolescence and functional obsolescence may both lead to the neglect of maintenance, and areas affected can deteriorate rapidly. Of the two, depreciation caused by economic obsolescence is the most difficult to deal with because it is based on extrinsic rather than intrinsic factors.

Rehabilitation or demolition?

With time, it may be necessary to determine when it is feasible to maintain or demolish and replace an obsolescent building. Repair and maintenance focuses on recognizing and diagnosing faults so as to extend the building's life, whereas rehabilitation involves conversion and modernization of buildings beyond the routine maintenance of cleaning or replacing defective parts. It involves improvements such as an additional bedroom, bathroom, new garage or kitchen extension. Rehabilitation can be applied to areas as well as individual buildings: for example, it may be more economic to install waterborne sanitation to a housing estate that previously used pit latrines or to provide children's play spaces when none existed, than to engage in wholesale demolition. Again, it is a question of choice based on the proper allocation of resources and the prediction of results. The factors that will influence the outcome include the soundness of the building, the anticipated residual life, the adaptability of the existing layout, planning regulations, construction costs, costs of finance, rent levels, and likely maintenance costs. Some of the main considerations will be:

Physical condition
1. The first priority is the repair and restoration of structural and weather-enclosing elements. What life expectation can be anticipated after rehabilitation? How does this match user requirements?
2. What is the condition of materials and components, including damp-proofing and insulation? What materials can be salvaged for re-use?
3. Are internal and external services adequate? Can drains and other mains services cope with requirements after rehabilitation. If not, is salvage and re-use possible?

Space gain and space change
1. Within the building envelope. What is the total volume? Are floor to floor heights adequate (or excessive)? Is there scope for extra accommodation? Can the roof space be used? What limitations are there to restructuring?
2. Outside the building envelope. Can spaces between buildings be filled? Can the building be extended by annexes or extensions? Can extra storeys be added? Is the site large enough for new buildings to be added to improve the development? What extra space requirements will be generated by new activities, for example car parking, servicing, refuse storage and collection?
3. Should the area be reduced, or outbuildings be demolished to achieve a more compact and viable scheme?

Architectural character
1. What fabric should be kept? Is there a range of priorities from features 'to be kept at all costs' to those 'to be kept if possible'?
2. Does the building need restoring to a previous state which was more satisfactory/attractive than its present condition?
3. What aesthetic rules can and should be observed – including massing, details, angles of roofs, eave heights and materials?

Flexibility
1. Can space be articulated so as to permit a change of use? Can services be zoned and structured to allow for future growth and change?

Economic factors

1. Whatever the weightings of these technical considerations, the essential question to ask is how much it is worth spending on improvement compared to redevelopment. Nierstrasz[1] has suggested a method for determining when it is feasible to maintain or rehabilitate or demolish and replace a building.

As with modernization and demolition or reconstruction, the test is to compare modernization with rebuilding on the same site in terms of income receivable from the property or the present value of the building before and after modernization. The decision criterion is:

income after modernization = income after rebuilding

or

$$B(1+y)(at+m) = B(1+s)p + Bt(ap+m)$$

where B = value of existing structure before modernization

at = annuity factor $\left(\dfrac{i}{1-(1+i)^{-t}} \right)$

i = rate of interest

t = period of depreciation

ap = annuity factor with period of depreciation 50 years

s = cost of demolition expressed in B

m = annual expenditure on maintenance and taxes as part of the value B

f = cost of reconstruction expressed in value B

y = cost of modernization as part of value B of existing structure

The advantage of this formula is that with the exception of t, all relevant factors are expressed in terms of B, the value of the existing building before modernization. The other advantage is that since the comparison is between the modernization and replacement of a new building on the same site, the value of the site may be omitted on both sides of the equation. It may also be necessary to demolish a building if planning regulations have permitted rezoning to allow for greater density. There could also be a case of change of use which allows for the construction of higher income-earning projects than those currently allowed.

---

[1] F.H.J. Nierstrasz, 'Some Economic Aspects of Maintenance, Modernization and Replacement,' *Research on Maintenance and Modernization* (CIF Proceedings, Rotterdam, 1979).

For example, a site which was originally reserved for single-storey dwellings may be rezoned and the authorities will permit the alternatives of apartment blocks or commercial development. The value of the site after rezoning may be much higher than the value that could be achieved with the existing building.

CHAPTER 3

Maintenance Procedures for an Organization

Types of maintenance

Maintenance is defined as work involving the repair or restoration of a building to its original equivalent condition. It may be classified in many ways, but three of the most useful for management purposes are as follows:

By the size and nature of the works to be executed

1. Major maintenance to include each item of expenditure of the building fabric in excess of say US$2,500.
2. Minor maintenance to include each item of expenditure less than say US$2,500.
3. Maintenance of essential services to include preventive maintenance and repairs to electrical and mechanical installations and equipment such as lifts, air-conditioning systems, fire prevention services, generators, electrical wiring and plumbing.

According to the process of maintenance

1. Planned preventive maintenance. Work directed to the prevention of failure of a facility; this may include service contracts for the regular inspection and servicing of equipment.
2. Planned corrective maintenance. Work to replace or restore a facility to an acceptable standard; this may include reroofing, rewiring a building or simply replacing a door, so that the building continues to operate as intended.
3. Unplanned maintenance. Work resulting from unforeseen breakdown or damage due to external causes; such works are accidental and may include power failure, broken waterpipes or vandalized building facilities.

According to an expenditure budget

1. Cyclical maintenance. This includes items which regularly recur and must be carried out on a routine basis to maintain the structural characteristics of the building or to maintain the building as a suitable working environment. An example is painting and decoration, which should be carried out

regularly to protect wooden and metal components from rot, rust and decay. It is foolish to economize too much on cyclical maintenance, as this can lead to a much heavier eventual expenditure on major repairs or even replacement.
2. Occasional items. Some activities which fall into the category of repairs and maintenance will be carried out only when inspection reveals a serious structural or other fault. For example, the roof on a particular building may frequently leak during the rainy season, so that it requires almost continuous minor repairs. The point will come where it is cheaper to renew the complete roof structure, and this may in fact be treated as a 'capital' rather than a 'revenue' item.

Figure 3.1

Planned maintenance
The maintenance management process may be classified into two complementary and interacting systems namely, the schedule system and the contingency system. The schedule system of maintenance, commonly referred to as 'planned maintenance', consists of two mutually balanced components: planned preventive maintenance and planned corrective maintenance. Both must be organized with forethought, control and records, but their nature is different.

In the case of preventive maintenance, each item of work is identified some time before failure or deviation of the facility from an acceptable standard. Corrective maintenance differs in that restoration to the acceptable standard is required, and usually corrective maintenance must have a prior claim on available resources. In terms of 'duty of care' (derived from patient care), preventive maintenance would be similar to

41

works carried out by community health workers and administrative or preventive medicine. Corrective maintenance would be analogous to the administration of curative medicine in hospitals to patients already afflicted.

Whether preventive or corrective, planned maintenance requires a policy of observed defects in the same way that doctors and health visitors examine and follow-up cases of patients. The defects so identified for rectification can be grouped and a decision made as to when they should be rectified. This will allow for the allocation of resources in the most effective and efficient manner.

The contingency system

The alternative maintenance system is the contingency system, also known as unplanned maintenance, which is based on a policy of waiting until a complaint is received from the user before taking action, in the same manner that hospitals would administer cases in their casualty departments. In many developing countries, the contingency system is the most common programme of maintenance adopted by public authorities. In many cases, all works classed as minor are carried out by direct labour on a contingency basis, while major works are normally carried out by contractors. This system of maintenance does not rest on the concept of duty of care, since the authorities wait for users to report complaints. Unfortunately, in many cases users delay reporting defects until the buildings have deteriorated seriously, or they may only report those defects that affect the internal use of the buildings such as leaking roofs or taps. The effect of the contingency system is that the vital tasks of inspection and planning for building maintenance is entrusted to untrained amateurs.

Maintenance criteria

While the physical characteristics of a building that derive from design and construction largely determine maintenance budgets, management and organizational considerations are also significant. Studies carried out by the Bath University of Technology in the UK identified the following factors[1]:

1. Physical characteristics of the building, that is, technical criteria.
2. Organizational considerations such as hierarchy, personality and knowledge of the person in charge of building maintenance, as well as the detail and formality of the budget process.

1. Bath University of Technology, *BMCIS Feasibility study* (June 1969).

3. Policy considerations including the significance of maintenance for the public image of the organization in the light of
past and current uses of the buildings.
4. Economic criteria which is the extent to which building
maintenance is regarded as a factor in the total problem of
property management and the organization's attitude to
property as an asset required to provide economic returns on
investment.
5. Financial considerations, that is, the level of profitability of
the organization, the size of the direct labour-force, and the
levels of previous expenditure.
6. Environmental criteria such as the general economic climate
and the system of tenure.

Technical and non-technical criteria

The factors outlined above may be divided into technical or non-
technical criteria. What are the key non-technical criteria, and
what is their effect on the level of maintenance budgets?
Economic and financial considerations such as questions of
return on investment and profitability are certainly relevant to
commercial and industrial organizations where profit maximization is an overriding motive. However, the philosophy of profit
maximization is, in many respects, inappropriate for public
buildings. The least profitable buildings, such as civic buildings
and government institutions provided for service to the public,
would be the most dilapidated and yet progressively less money
would be spent on their maintenance.

Where policy considerations override technical criteria,
maintenance budgets are often the first to suffer. For instance,
where maintenance budgets have to be approved by local
councils, budgets are often pruned in favour of more pressing
services such as the provision of health or education. The same
exercise is carried out by central government during budget
cuts. It is also possible that building maintenance is considered
less important than new construction, so that fewer resources
will have to be made available for maintenance. Whatever the
quality of maintenance management, inadequate resources
imply that buildings will be badly maintained.

It is a fair generalization to state that technical criteria are
usually undervalued. Essentially, technical considerations
depend on the age of the building, as well as the quality and
standard of past maintenance. The aim should be to keep the
building as close as possible to the original standard or currently
acceptable standard. As suggested earlier, the guiding principle

in adopting technical criteria as a basis for maintenance standard is the concept of duty of care.

The concept of duty of care

Where maintenance budgets are set on technical criteria, namely the physical needs of the building, the guiding principle is to set and agree an appropriate standard of structural and decorative repair. This should at least match, but may very well exceed, the statutory requirements. It is therefore necessary to determine some objective levels that will accommodate as far as possible the various requirements of those with an interest in the building. This process could be likened to the doctor's approach to a patient in a hospital whose need of treatment depends on the diagnosis of his state of health. Using this analogy, there are in practice three basic principles of patient care[2]. The first is light care, to include treatment of minor cuts and bruises, as well as administration of drugs at regular intervals. Secondly, there is intermediary care, to include care associated with pre- or post-operative situations of less serious nature. Finally, intensive care, which includes the continuous and detailed monitoring and treatment of patients' conditions, when suffering from critical injuries.

These levels of care are used as the basis for determining the necessary resources in terms of equipment and manpower in the nursing profession. This scale could be used in building maintenance, provided it is known what is to be maintained within the building, and what operation is necessary for the required remedy. Maintenance operations such as cleaning, patching or replacement would need to be classified into levels of care; while maintenance management programmes of preventive, corrective or emergency/contingency maintenance should contain levels of care intended by each programme. Theoretically, the higher the order of the degree of care, the greater the maintenance task, and presumably the higher the expenditure.

The level of care required by a building depends on a variety of maintenance generators which act upon the building and erode the standards. These may include climatic exposure, user activities and changing tests and technology. The rates at which these generators create the need for maintenance depends on the quality of the design as well as the quality of the construction. Design encompasses a wide range of activities including choice of materials, decision about size and layout as well as the implied choice of the method of construction.

2. A. Wahlin, *et al, Intensive care* (John Wiley and Sons, 1972).

Levels of intent in building maintenance

R. Lee[3], in discussing standards for building maintenance, distinguishes three broad levels of intent which are related to the environmental effect on users of a building. There is the lowest level, so that the immediate environment should neither be uncomfortable nor directly harmful; then the middle level, so that the environment should be such as to minimize unproductive effort at work or maximize output and lastly the highest level, so that the environment should promote the actual well-being of the users as well as their sensation of well-being.

This classification is considered in terms of the environmental effect on user activities. The environmental subsystems considered are visual, thermal and acoustic. The visual environment includes daylight and artificial lighting, therefore it is suggested that maintenance should be carried out to ensure that adequate lighting is achieved in the buildings as originally planned. The thermal environment is considered in terms of ambient room temperature; it is suggested that the control of this temperature should depend on the correct operation and maintenance of service installations. This presupposes that mechanical systems have been installed for ventilation, heating and cooling; a situation which is not true in many tropical countries where thermal comfort can often be obtained more cheaply and effectively through natural air movement. The acoustic environment is considered in terms of sound installation, and here good maintenance can assist in reducing the ambient noise level.

Performance elements

The Local Government Operations Research Unit in the UK has used the 'performance elements' concept in determining the maintenance needs for hospital buildings[4]. Using this concept, a list was drawn up of the elements of the building fabric that are most important in relation to maintenance so as to keep buildings functional. Each element is described in terms of its physical appearance through various periods of its life. For instance, a flat roof may pass through four distinct stages:

3. R. Lee, *Building maintenance management*, second edition (1981).
4. R.G. Howel, *Development of Economic Policies for Hospital Building Maintenance* (Local Government Operations Research Unit, Royal Institute of Public Administration, UK, 1970).

State A – no visible defects
State B – no leaking but some blistering
State C – slight cracking of blisters and small leaks
State D – perished with open joints, extensive cracking, tearing and leaking.

It could be that various parts of an element may deteriorate at different rates, in which case it is possible to describe which percentage of the element falls within each state. For instance, when a roof is new it should fall wholly in State A, that is, 100 per cent of the roof will be without defects. After four years, for instance, some parts of the roof may be blistered, though actually not leaking, while the rest is still relatively unworn. This is state B, and some 40 per cent of the roof may be in this state. The roof may begin to leak when it is eight years old, in which case its condition will be a mixture of states A, B and C. The percentage areas in these states could be 30, 60 and 10 respectively.

Having determined the physical state of each element, the next step is to calculate the amount of labour and materials required at each state of deterioration in order to forecast the cost of maintenance and repair at each stage. With the cost known, it is then possible to develop a maintenance strategy for the building element, to determine whether it is cheaper to patch and defer major expenditure or renew it at current costs.

This assumes that the life of the element can be forecast with some accuracy. Where life expectancy is not known, the concept of average annual cost is useful for purposes of comparison. At each stage the accumulated maintenance costs of each element are added to its original cost. The sum of the two gives the total cost of the element to the user at that time: this figure, divided by the age, gives the average annual cost of the element if it is to be replaced at this stage. This concept can be used for maintenance allocation as well as comparing costs in the use of alternative materials.

Table 3.1 Example of inspection data

Element	Present condition	Condition by next inspection	Cost of renewal ($)	Cost of repair ($)
External painting	A	B	10	–
Asbestos sheet roof	C	D	100	80

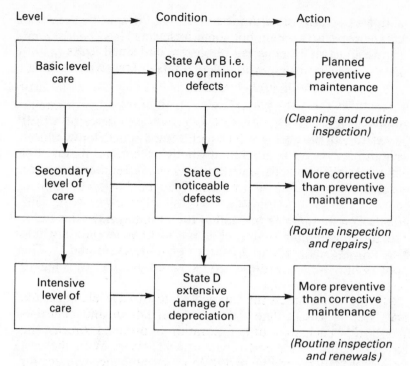

Figure 3.2 *Levels of maintenance care*

Inspection

To determine the stage of deterioration of the elements which make up a particular building it is necessary periodically to carry out a visual inspection of all elements scheduled to require work in the coming year and inspect closely any elements that show unusual signs of deterioration. For each element, inspection data should be set out in tabular form and regularly updated as shown in Table 3.1.

'Present condition' refers to the state as seen, while 'condition by next inspection' assumes a normal rate of deterioration. 'Cost of renewal' refers to renewing the whole element immediately, while 'cost of repair' refers to the cost of repairing the element during the next time interval if postponed. Inspections should be carried out at regular intervals according to the management system adopted by the particular organization.

Relevance of concept of duty of care

The acceptance of the concept of duty of care in building maintenance is a measure of the organization's commitment to

47

adopt a professional attitude to meeting the specific needs of a given property throughout its economic life. These needs should be established during the design stage, then subsequently monitored and re-appraised regularly throughout the period of use, as conditions may change or accidents may occur calling for departures from the plan. However, the level of care must be related to the likely conditions or building states previously determined through a system of programmed maintenance. Figure 3.2 is a diagrammatic model relating the levels of maintenance required to the building at various stages in its life cycle.

Basis of maintenance budgeting for an organization

As the maintenance manager comes to draw up the budget for the coming year, he or she has to take account of the general policy of their organization. Some of the factors which have to be remembered include:

Demand for maintenance
Resources
Standards of service
Need for regular maintenance
Standards costs
Productivity
Use classes of buildings.

Demand for maintenance

If the use of a building is to be intensified it is likely that a higher expenditure will be needed to keep the required standards. In factory premises or workshops, new processes might give rise to greater demand. In a shop or office, the organization may decide to provide higher standards to improve relations with customers.

Resources

The budget will be affected by the overall financial resources available to the organization. A company or firm will be limited by the amount of its working capital and the levels of cash flow and profits. A government department will be limited by the funds that can be raised and allocated by the Ministry of Finance. However, it is the responsibility of the maintenance manager to calculate the level of expenditure that would be adequate in accordance with accepted standards of safety and the organization's general policy. If a lower level of expenditure is adopted for reasons of general financial stringency, this fact should be clearly stated so that higher levels of management will

48

realize the implications, and not complain needlessly at a later stage that the buildings are not as well maintained as they would wish.

Standards of service

One of the major problems facing any maintenance manager is the large number of demands placed upon him for repairs and redecoration, and the difficulty of allocating priorities when the urgency of the various claims seems to be equal. This is a particularly difficult problem where house maintenance is concerned, and there is a danger that the manager will be accused of favouritism whichever job is chosen as a priority. A useful guide-line is to break down the allowance for maintenance into sums for each house type, to show clearly how much money is available for maintenance on each during the year. If the amount allocated in the budget is not enough to meet the needs, some kind of rationing system will have to be operated or, where maintenance is planned on a regular cycle, the period of the cycle must be increased. For example, painting may be carried out every four years instead of every three years.

Need for regular maintenance

Wherever possible maintenance should be carried out on a preventive basis, with specific time cycles allocated for each particular task. In many countries, safety legislation requires regular maintenance of items such as lifting tackle, but jobs like external painting should also be carried out regularly if the structure is to remain sound and keep its value. Unfortunately, there is always a temptation to extend the maintenance cycle when money is short, although this leads to an ever-increasing backlog of work so that it becomes increasingly difficult for the maintenance department to catch up with their schedules and bring the buildings up to an acceptable standard. The maintenance manager is in a stronger position to secure sufficient funds to fulfil his duties properly if he prepares fully costed programmes for cyclical repairs and maintenance from which a budget can be accurately built up.

Standard costs

Where repetitive costs are involved, standard costing techniques can be very helpful in improving the accuracy of budget forecasts. The standards must be based on realistic assumptions of output and productivity and should make allowances for fixed overhead costs. These standards will also be of great value in estimating costs for additional work that may be required from time to time.

49

Productivity

The resources needed to undertake a given volume of work in a labour-intensive activity such as building maintenance is highly dependant upon the productivity of the labour-force. This can be very difficult to assess in maintenance work, due to the huge variability of the tasks to be performed. However, by using standard costing techniques, supported by the recruitment and training of reliable foremen and supervisors, the maintenance manager can achieve steady improvements in productivity and the quality of the service provided.

Figure 3.3

Classifying uses of buildings

It will be of help to divide the properties into a series of uses, since different types of building have different needs for standard, regular and urgent maintenance. Most maintenance managers will only have to look after a few of these categories. For example, a Ministry of Works may have workshops, stores, offices and some residential property. A Ministry of Education may have offices and residential buildings as well as its schools and colleges.

In addition, some types of building may have to be maintained at particular times or periods of the year so that the work does not interfere with their operational requirements. In general, schools are redecorated in holiday periods so that the teaching programme is not disrupted. Repair and maintenance work on factory buildings may have to be done at weekends to avoid interruptions. Special arrangements may have to be made in the case of shops and supermarkets so that regular customers do not change their shopping habits because their usual shop is closed for a period.

50

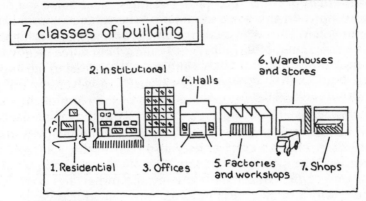

Figure 3.4

Classifying needs

Any classification must be rather arbitrary, but seven classes of building with comments on their general needs are outlined on the following pages.

Residential

This classification includes houses, bungalows, flats and domestic quarters. The occupier of the property will normally pay a rental partly to cover depreciation of the property and interest on the capital value, but also to cover the costs of regular repairs and maintenance. The latter element could be adjusted to cover actual costs, so that repairs and maintenance could become broadly self-financing.

The objective should be to provide reasonably comfortable living surroundings. Fixtures and fittings may need to be more

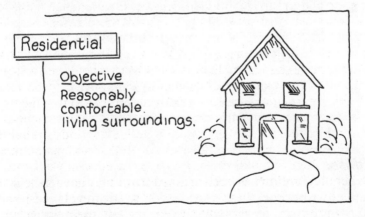

Figure 3.5

51

robust than in owner-occupied dwellings, since some families may subject them to harsh treatment. Where difficult, 'problem' families have to be housed, it may be necessary to reserve a particular group of dwellings for them, where damages will be less serious. Careful thought should be given as to which items will be repaired by the authority and which will be the responsibility of the occupier.

Institutional

The category covers a broad range of institutional buildings including schools, universities, hospitals, health centres and libraries. The government normally commissions the building and one of the Ministries is usually the owner and occupier. There will normally be an attempt to standardize designs in order to reduce construction costs, and this can lower maintenance costs, since operations can be made routine, so maintenance staff should be faced with fewer unexpected problems.

At the design stage, steps should be taken to incorporate features, components and materials that will minimize repairs and decorations, using easily-cleaned and hard-wearing decorative materials. Unfortunately what usually happens is that the maintenance manager is unable to influence the design, and therefore has to gradually introduce improvements when redecorations and replacements become due.

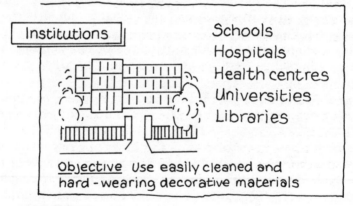

Figure 3.6

Offices

Where legislation has been enacted covering standards of safety and environment, these must be complied with. However, it is also important to provide a pleasant environment in which employees can give their best. A colour scheme using light-coloured finishes will improve conditions for office employees, since they will find it difficult to work effectively in a dark building.

Sound-proofing can be very important, too, as the sound of typing, for example, can be heard through flimsy partitions and can interrupt telephone calls or important business discussions. In large offices, it is helpful to ensure that all rooms are clearly and logically numbered so that visitors can find their way around without difficulty.

Figure 3.7

Halls and places of assembly

This category includes theatres, cinemas, sports stadia, churches and other buildings where large groups of people meet for various purposes. The maintenance manager who has responsibility for this group of buildings should concentrate on two main areas of priority. The first is where the building is used for a commercial purpose, such as film shows at a cinema; he will have to keep the building in a condition that will attract paying customers. This will mean regular cleaning and decoration so that the building presents a pleasant, clean and tidy appearance. The second case refers to the danger of panic where large crowds assemble; thus specific attention must be given to balconies, barriers and fire escapes in order to ensure that structural safety is maintained and any defective elements are promptly replaced. The need to be able to vacate the building rapidly in the case of fire or other emergencies means that escape doors should be regularly checked and no equipment or materials should be left or stored in corridors.

53

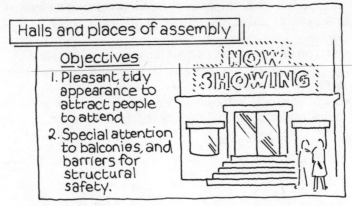

Figure 3.8

Factories and workshops

The prime duty is to satisfy statutory requirements. However, it is also important to provide an acceptable working environment in which workers feel encouraged to maintain good levels of productivity. In premises such as machine shops or foundries, which are subject to particularly heavy wear, the regularity of maintenance inspections should be increased.

Care should be taken in siting additional machinery so that there is adequate working space around it for operation and maintenance. Advice should be sought on the design of foundations for heavy machinery so that there is no danger of overstressing the existing building.

The maintenance staff should make sure that gangways between machinery are clearly marked with white lines, and that the operatives do not leave parts or materials in gangway areas.

Figure 3.9

54

Figure 3.10

Warehouses and stores

The main requirement here is to ensure that the stability and working life of the structure and its elements are maintained. Usually, only a small number of people will be employed in relation to the area occupied by the building. Special attention should be given to the provision of suitable environmental conditions if perishables are to be stored.

Where mechanical handling devices such as conveyor systems or fork-lift trucks are to be used in an existing building, it may be necessary to consult a qualified structural engineer to check that the building is sufficiently strong to withstand the additional loads.

Figure 3.11

Shops

In addition to maintaining the strength and stability of the structure, the maintenance manager should ensure that the premises are neatly decorated and kept clean and tidy. A clean and attractive appearance encourages potential customers to enter a shop initially and then return to make regular purchases.

If the shop is used for the sale of food, special attention should be given to ensuring that the food can be properly stored so that it will not deteriorate due to heat or attacks by rodents or insects. A further consideration may be the danger of burglaries, in which case the maintenance manager may have to install shutters, steel bars or burglar alarms to deter potential thieves.

General considerations

The main difference in the maintenance programme will be seen in the levels and standards of internal maintenance. External maintenance and structural requirements will be similar for all classifications of use, although the actual amount of work to be done will naturally depend upon the age of the building, the materials and type of construction. However, the variations in requirements for internal maintenance are such that it is usually best to prepare separate master lists and plans for the various use classes. Apart from a planning advantage, it is also helpful to separate the various use classes for budgeting and general accountancy purposes, so that the maintenance costs for various types of building can be correctly assessed.

Before a full maintenance budget can be prepared, it is first necessary to clarify the maintenance programmes for all properties involved, leading to the preparation of a master maintenance plan.

PART TWO
MANAGEMENT

CHAPTER 4
Costing and Financial Control

Whether the organization concerned with maintenance is a large and busy public works department or a small jobbing builder, there will be a need for top management to set the policy and ensure that progress is properly monitored. Great care must be given to setting up a suitable cost recording and reporting system so that it is not overcumbersome to operate yet provides essential information for monitoring past performance and improving future budgets and policies.

Motivation is a further factor of crucial interest to top management. Maintenance managers and their staff often suffer from a steadily sapped morale as their only contact with other staff or the public occurs when something has gone wrong in one of the buildings for which they are responsible, and at other times they are barely tolerated as a necessary but unproductive nuisance. This may be partly due to the lack of objective criteria in the work area of building maintenance. An effective budgeting system covering planning for costs, liquidity and capital expenditure can make a useful contribution to dealing with this problem by making clear that the maintenance function performs an essential task and that its performance can be measured.

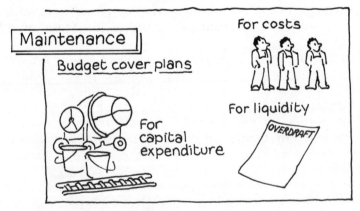

Figure 4.1

58

Measurement is one of the keys to good management and, since engineers and managers rely on numeracy, activities that are not measured (either because they are thought to be unmeasurable or because they are not thought to be worth measuring) tend to be undervalued. This is understandable since activities must be measurable if plans are to be quantified and actions monitored and evaluated. If the maintenance manager wishes to ensure that his problems and achievements are appreciated by top management, s/he should give careful attention to devising and operating an appropriate system of budgetary control.

The general process of budgeting has been compared to the routine followed by a ship's captain who is about to undertake a voyage from one port to another. When s/he has been told the destination s/he will start to plan the route, taking into account the ship, the type of cargo, tides and possible climatic problems. During the voyage s/he consults the plans and records any unexpected happenings. If necessary s/he may even deviate from the planned route to take account of these. After the voyage s/he will compare the actual voyage with the plan, thus gaining in insight and experience. In the same way the maintenance manager, who also has to deal with many uncertainties, can use the budget as a yardstick and a guide in an effort to keep on course. The first step in setting budget figures is to install a proper system for cost recording and control.

Costing

Costs can be classified into three groups: committed costs, variable costs and managed costs.

Committed costs cover costs that cannot normally be altered during a particular accounting period as a fixed contract exists with a supplier, for example covering the lease of office equipment.

Variable or 'engineered' costs are closely related to the activity of the organization and their size is fairly closely related to the output of the unit. For example, labour and material costs for concreting on a large building site are likely to grow in proportion to the quantity of concrete to be poured. It is possible, in theory at least, to measure the work content accurately and establish precise costs for a given level of activity.

Managed costs are uncommitted and are not directly related to the volume of activity, but are specifically authorized at the discretion of the management. Since all decisions on managed costs are of a 'one-off' nature, they are a matter of judgement on the part of the maintenance manager.

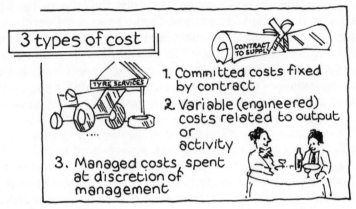

3 types of cost

1. Committed costs fixed by contract
2. Variable (engineered) costs related to output or activity
3. Managed costs, spent at discretion of management

Figure 4.2

Committed costs are the easiest both to identify and to handle, since they are defined by the conditions of the contract entered into by the supplier or contractor. Any variation in cost will either be carried by the contractor or be absorbed within a 'contingency item' in the contract. For this reason some organizations prefer to rely on outside contractors rather than a direct labour-force under their own control. However, there are other financial advantages that can result from carrying out work by direct labour since, assuming the same regular levels of efficiency and output can be achieved, the profit margin that would have been required by the private contractor will accrue to the benefit of the employer. In addition, a direct labour-force can be deployed more flexibly than the employees of a private contractor, who may require a variation order before the programme of work is changed.

Unfortunately, there is no scientific method by which any given type of cost can be clearly categorized as always being an 'engineered cost' or always being a 'managed cost'. The difference between them is in their usefulness in evaluating performance. Since engineered costs are directly related to output, if the labour cost is budgeted as 40 per cent of output, a labour cost of 38 per cent would be an improvement but a labour cost of 45 per cent would suggest that something was going wrong.

Performance on managed costs, however, is not as easy to

judge objectively, particularly with regard to the maintenance function. If a sum of £25,000 is allocated for 'general building maintenance to workshops' and only £19,000 is spent it may mean that the maintenance manager has done a good job. But it may also mean that s/he has not bothered to carry out the work properly or that the original estimate (or guesstimate!) was too high.

Managers usually perform best when their activities are measurable and their performance can be realistically evaluated, and consequently it is usually a basic aim of management to move costs wherever possible from the 'managed' category to the 'engineered' category. Many accountants seem to see no prospect of switching maintenance costs in this way, so they despairingly lump all maintenance expenditure into the category of managed costs. However, the search continues for ways of quantifying and rationalizing building maintenance costing procedures. This search is particularly important for larger organizations, where annual maintenance costs amount to substantial sums. The survey carried out by the Bath University of Technology for the UK Ministry of Public Building and Works suggested the following broad list of maintenance criteria:

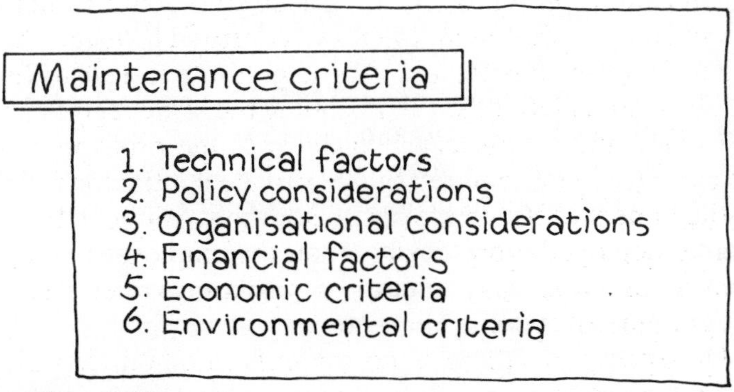

```
┌─────────────────────────────────────────────┐
│  ┌──────────────────────────┐                │
│  │ Maintenance criteria     │                │
│  └──────────────────────────┘                │
│        1. Technical factors                  │
│        2. Policy considerations              │
│        3. Organisational considerations      │
│        4. Financial factors                  │
│        5. Economic criteria                  │
│        6. Environmental criteria             │
│                                              │
└─────────────────────────────────────────────┘
```

Figure 4.3

Technical factors
Age of buildings
Nature of design (degree of in-built maintenance)
Material specification
Past standard of maintenance, including regularity of treatment, quality of work and any backlog of essential work
Cost of postponing maintenance.

Policy considerations
Prestige – whether maintenance standard is in keeping with 'image' of organization without being overlavish
Nature of past and current usage of building
Extent to which productivity of employees may be reduced by poor working environment (or enhanced by good).

Organizational considerations
Position of building maintenance department in the organizational hierarchy
Personality of maintenance manager
Knowledge and experience of decision-maker in top management
Degree of detail and formality of the budgeting process.

Financial factors
Level of profitability of organization or (in the case of a public body) resources allocated by Ministry of Finance
Cash-flow availability during financial year
Timing of works programme and its effect upon cash flow
Size of direct labour-force and its financial implications
Prices and general levels of cost
Level of previous expenditure and its cost effectiveness plus a factor for inflation together with an addition to cover any expansion of premises or new activity that may increase wear and tear on buildings.

Economic criteria
Extent to which building maintenance is seen as a factor in the total problem of property management
Organizations attitude to property as an asset required to provide an economic return on investment.

Environmental criteria
The general economic climate
The system of tenure
Environmental changes.

Under this final heading, the physical position of the site is also important in relation to adjacent industry or social activity which may change. If the road by the building becomes a route to a football ground or if chemical attack from exhaust fumes increases, this may also alter maintenance requirements.

The weight to be attached to each of these criteria will of course vary from organization to organization. In some cases the need for maintenance is more or less directly related to the age of the building, but many soundly constructed old buildings are likely to give less trouble than flimsy new structures. In fact, one reason for keeping a close watch on maintenance budgets and costs is to 'feed back' lessons by the maintenance unit on materials and design features that give rise to high maintenance costs, so that they can be avoided in future structures.

Thus the costing system should be designed in such a way that any unusual item for 'general repairs' on a particular building is highlighted, so that it will lead the maintenance manager to ask the right questions. The first question should be 'Is this a normal and forecastable failure?' and the second 'How can we avoid, or at least delay, a similar failure in the future?'

Figure 4.4

In some cases s/he may decide that there is little that can be done to improve the performance of the existing building. However, the analysis will still have been useful since it will allow the maintenance manager to put forward a reasonable objection to any similar design feature in future buildings of the same type. If this is done in a systematic way over a period of years, the maintenance performance of the stock of buildings under the manager's control should progressively improve.

Setting up a costing system
The final objective of any costing system is to allow the manager to make objective decisions leading to effective cost control and then to a study of the possibilities for cost reduction. The system will only be useful if it improves the way in which tomorrow's problems are tackled, although the first step is to make clear how well or how badly previous decisions have worked out in practice.

The first function of a maintenance costing system is to provide a clear record of the running costs for a building or a group of buildings. To achieve this, all expenditure throughout the year must be collected into suitable expense centres according to location and type. This implies a suitable cost-coding system so that the many small individual costs involved in building maintenance can be collected together systematically from job-cards, time-sheets and stores' issue-notes.

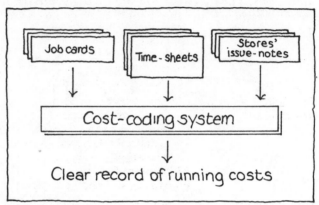

Figure 4.5

The design of an appropriate coding system is a vital task, and its structure must depend on the particular needs of an individual organization. It must, however, be both simple and clear, so that it can be applied without an army of clerical workers, and to allow the cost figures to be kept up to date, abstracted and compared with budget figures regularly. A typical system of cost-coding classification for maintenance expenditure on housing and buildings is given below.

Typical cost codes

Primary codes	Secondary codes
1. External decoration	
2. Internal decoration	
3. Main structure	31 Foundations and basements
	32 Frame
	33 External walls
	34 Roof structure
	35 Roof coverings
	36 Roof lights and glazing
	37 Gutters and rainwater pipes

64

	38 Windows
	39 External doors including glazing
4. Internal construction	41 Ground floors
	42 Upper floors
	43 Staircases and steps
	44 Internal walls – structural
	45 Partitions and partition walls
	46 Internal doors including glazing
5. Finishes and fittings	51 Ceiling finishes
	52 Wall finishes
	53 Floor finishes
	54 Joinery, shelves, etc.
	55 Ironmongery
	56 Miscellaneous fittings
6. Plumbing and sanitary services	61 Cold water service-pipes, tanks, cisterns and valves
	62 Hot water service-pipes, tanks, cylinder boilers, valves and insulation
	63 Sanitary fittings
	64 Waste, soil and vent-pipes
7. Mechanical services, heating and ventilating	71 Boilers, firing, flues
	72 Hot water distribution
	73 External water supply, treatment and storage
	74 Air conditioning, ventilation and refrigeration
	75 Lifts
	76 Workshop equipment
	77 Miscellaneous equipment
8. Electrical services	81 Generation
	82 Transmission and distribution
	83 Wiring, switch and control gear
	84 Appliances and fittings
	85 External lighting
	86 Lighting protection
	87 Kitchen equipment
9. External works	91 Roads, car parks, hardstandings
	92 Paths, playgrounds, paved areas
	93 Fences, walls and gates
	94 Drains and ditches
	95 Sewers and sewage disposal
	96 Water storage
	97 Gardens
	98 Miscellaneous external works

It is of course possible to achieve greater accuracy by adding tertiary codes, but this must be balanced against the increased overhead and staff costs that would be involved. Where, for example, it is suspected that certain types of flooring give rise to substantially higher maintenance costs than others, appropriate tertiary cost divisions will provide objective evidence over a period of time. In applying the cost-code allocation system, it is most important that costs for individual jobs are not duplicated, and are either applied to a single code number or split between codes on a suitable proportional basis.

The accuracy of a costing system is wholly dependant on the accuracy of the information upon which it is based. Thus a proper booking system for labour and materials is vital. All existing forms should be checked to make sure that they are adequate and provide all the information that is required. (It is also important to make sure that they do not waste the operative's time by asking for information that is *not* required). The basic forms will probably be *a daily labour allocation sheet*, showing the number of men in each gang employed on various tasks (Figure 6.16), *a materials sheet*, detailing the materials employed in each job (Figure 6.17) and *a job sheet*, describing the work carried out and detailing any additional expenses (Figure 6.18).

Figure 4.6

If the forms are very different from those currently in use in the organization, they should be explained to the foreman who will be required to complete them. Once the new forms are in use, it will be possible to start gathering the material for cost analysis, by collating the costs of labour and material into totals against each item in the cost code, summarized by location and type.

Comparison with estimates

Once the costs for an accounting period have been collated, they should be compared with the original estimates. It will be particularly important to look closely at those items where estimated costs have been exceeded, and to investigate the reasons for the excess. Where these figures differ widely from the estimate, it may be worthwhile to compare them with figures for previous years.

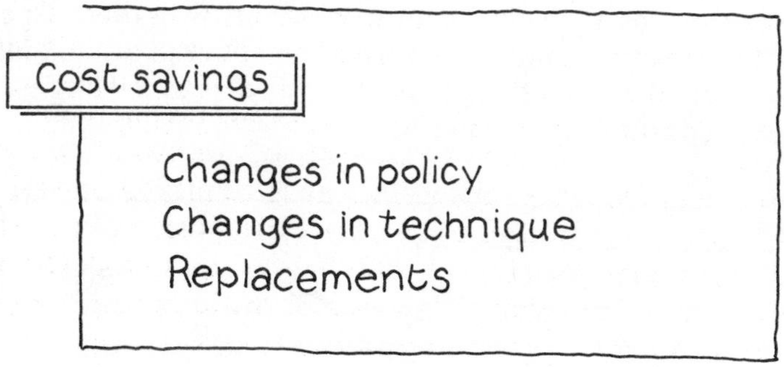

Figure 4.7

Cost-saving investigations

The next stage is to examine the possibilities for achieving cost savings, by changes in policy, technique or replacement of items which are giving rise to unacceptable maintenance or repair costs. Examples of changes which might lead to savings due to lower overall maintenance costs are:

1. Replacement of plant or equipment with high maintenance costs or which breaks down frequently, or which is not fully-used as it is not efficient.
2. Replacement of plant or equipment with high fuel costs.
3. Provision of additional plant and tools for maintenance.
4. Provision of automatic lighting controls to reduce electricity costs.

Besides allowing management to assess the possibilities for cost saving by policy changes on a realistic basis, cost figures should provide the basis for future revenue budgets.

Preparing the maintenance budget

A proper budgeting process is crucial to effective cost control on a continuing basis in all organizations, whether in the public or the private sector. It is also important that budgeting should not be a process that is simply left to the accountants, since it must be based on a proper technical appreciation of maintenance needs. A further factor is that the budget must be used as a working document throughout the year, and managers are more likely to work wholeheartedly to achieve budgets which they have put forward themselves than figures which have been imposed by others.

Since resources for maintenance are usually particularly scarce in developing countries, it is vital that they should be planned and used to the best possible advantage. The budget is the vital link in the chain of control which involves three aspects. First the communication of information about plans and intentions. Second, motivating people to achieve planned targets and finally, reporting performance.

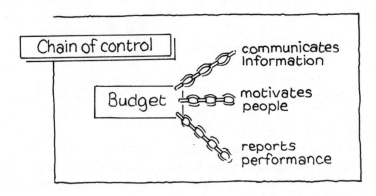

Figure 4.8

The third aspect leads to a continuing cycle of activity, in which the accuracy of plans and budgets should be steadily improved, leading to maintenance expenditure yielding greater benefits in the form of an improved working environment and buildings with a longer useful life. The basis for effective control of any activity must be careful planning, but accurate information is also needed as a guide.

Although a budget is naturally expressed in financial terms, these figures must be seen as an expression of human responsibilities since it is the maintenance manager and his staff who control operations, answer complaints and decide priorities. Although some maintenance managers feel that their experience is so great that they can make day to day decisions without guidance, the quality of all decisions can only be as good as the quality of the knowledge of the facts (or assumptions) upon which they are based. One of the most important functions of a budget is to provide a factual basis for control.

Figure 4.9

Financial planning is part of the overall planning of an organization covering the long term and the medium term, while budgetary control is concerned with the planning of operations in the relatively short term. The financial plan, which should include plans for the long-term provision of funds for repair and maintenance of buildings, will project long-term plans for the organization in financial terms. Within the framework of the financial plan, a budgetary control system should be operated to ensure that detailed plans are prepared for the current year of the long-term financial plan.

In most cases, the budget will run for a period of one year. Budgeting beyond a period of one year can be difficult, particularly for repairs and maintenance, which can be very difficult to forecast. There must, however, be much shorter 'control' periods – when actual costs and performance are measured and compared with an appropriate proportion of the budgeted figure. If the maintenance manager were to leave comparing the actual costs with the budget until the end of the financial year, it would then be much too late to take corrective action. Thus the budget is broken down into a series of control

69

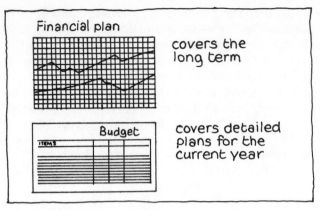

Figure 4.10

periods: weekly, monthly or at the most three-monthly, at the end of each of which the actual cost and performance is compared with those forecast or implied in the budget.

At the end of each control period, the manager should examine the figures and take particular note of those which vary greatly from the budget. If costs are higher than budgeted, s/he should determine the reasons: it may simply be that the operative's performance is at fault and that productivity must be improved. In the emergency repairs' category, which is notoriously difficult to forecast accurately, it may simply be that an abnormally large item has had to be dealt with in this particular control period. The third possibility is that the original budgeted figure was too low. In this case, the budget may have to be revised upwards, although it may be possible to make com-

Figure 4.11

pensating savings on items where actual costs are lower than budget, so that the overall total remains the same.

It is very important that this analysis should be carried out as soon as possible after the figures for the particular control period become available. The longer the activities of the department go on unchecked, the greater will be the danger of serious overspending or failing to complete the planned programme of work. There are a great many ways of analysing costs and expenditure, but the aim should always be to present the facts in such a way that they point to a sensible decision on the way in which resources are to be used.

Maintenance plans and programmes
Although maintenance plans and programmes for a large group of buildings of various ages, materials and types of construction may well be very complex, the objective of the plans and programmes is simple. It is to answer three basic questions:

What is to be maintained?
How is it to be maintained?
When should it be maintained?

The answer to the first question is usually 'all the buildings used by the organization', but the answer to the second question will depend on use, class and the physical nature of the building itself. It can only be answered satisfactorily after careful examination of each building, leading preferably to a job specification which will describe fully the tasks to be carried out at each maintenance inspection interval. A full system of job specifications will take time to formulate, but will be a vital aid to effective planned maintenance by ensuring that:

1. The task or job is carried out in the manner intended.
2. The possibility of a particular item being forgotten (perhaps endangering structural safety) is minimized.
3. Acceptable levels of wear and deterioration before repainting, repair or replacement are clearly defined.
4. The craftsman or operative understands what is required of him or her.
5. The work will always be carried out in the same way, so that the performance of materials and components can be objectively compared.
6. All workers carry out tasks in the same way, easing calculations for work study or incentive bonus purposes.
7. A reference standard is available in that additional buildings of the same type can be rapidly brought into the system as soon as they are built or acquired.

```
┌─────────────────────────────┐
│  Job specifications    ║     │
├──────────────┐              │
│  ensure...   │              │
│  1. Job is carried out as intended.
│  2. Items are not forgotten.
│  3. Definition of acceptable wear
│      and tear.
│  4. Craftsmen know what to do.
│  5. Materials performance can be
│      compared.
│  6. Easier work study calculations.
│  7. A record of standards for reference.
└──────────────────────────────┘
```

Figure 4.12

Each job specification should give certain details including:

1. The number or title of the particular building.
2. Its address or location.
3. The maintenance schedule reference number.
4. The job specification reference number.
5. The frequency of maintenance.
6. The trades (for instance carpenter, mason, painter) required to carry out the work.
7. The specific details of the work to be inspected and carried out.
8. Any special tools and equipment required.
9. Working drawings, manuals and specifications available.
10. Safety procedures to be followed.

The frequency of major maintenance and repair works will depend on the type and use of the building, but will probably be based on a maintenance cycle of three, four or five years. Whichever cycle is chosen, it must be used as the basis for all detailed planning, so that no buildings are forgotten and allowed to slip into serious disrepair.

Once the maintenance manager has decided on a suitable cycle of maintenance for the buildings for which s/he is responsible, s/he can prepare a master maintenance plan which will show the work to be carried out in each successive year. Where many different types of building have to be repaired and maintained, it is possible to have different maintenance cycles for different types of building. However, it is generally preferable to decide on an appropriate period between maintenance inspections and apply this universally.

The master maintenance plan should be a simple document, listing the properties to be maintained on the left and giving a series of columns, one for each financial year, so that the maintenance inspection dates for each year can be clearly indicated. It may be helpful to split each yearly column into two so that the date on which work on any particular building has been completed can also be clearly indicated. An example of a typical maintenance master plan for government buildings is shown in Figure 4.13:

Building	1977/78	78/79	79/80	80/81	81/82	82/83	83/84	84/85	85/86	86/87
Ministry of Works main office	x 16/7					x				
Ministry of Works district office		x 30/5					x			
Mechanical workshop			x 8/5					x		
Main store				x 1/9					x	
Training centre					x 2/8					x
Main garage	x 20/8					x				
Joinery workshop	x 1/2					x				
House 1		x 15/6					x			
House 2		x 25/7					x			
House 3			x 20/7				x			

Figure 4.13 *Typical maintenance master plan*

The crosses indicate the financial year in which maintenance is due, and the dates are filled in to show when the work to be carried out following the maintenance inspection has been completed. When preparing the maintenance master plan, the maintenance manager will take care to ensure that the work to be done is reasonably balanced between one year and another. This leads to a steady work-load, and allows the manager to recruit a full-time permanent maintenance crew as well as ensuring that the budget should not fluctuate from year to year (apart from provision for wage and price increases).

The maintenance master plan, like all plans, is only useful if it is employed as a working document. If a five-year cycle of inspection, maintenance and repair has been decided on, this

73

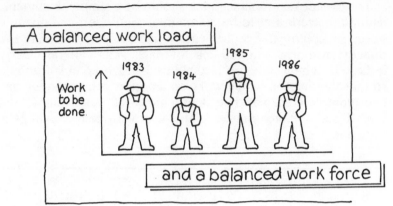

Figure 4.14

must be worked to. Otherwise, the backlog from one year will be carried forward to the next, making that year's task much more difficult to achieve and requiring additional financial resources which may not be made available. Once this point has been reached, it is all too easy to allow the situation to get completely out of control, so that maintenance planning ceases altogether and the maintenance gangs return to the chaos of reacting to complaints as they arise.

Figure 4.15

A further important point is that when the time comes for a building to be dealt with, the work should be completed in one operation. This is a good reason for setting up a comprehensive inspection system, so that the clerk-of-works will examine the building in detail and decide on the work to be done before the maintenance gang start their work. Apart from the fact that discontinuous operations are usually uneconomic as well as inconvenient to building users or occupiers, a very bad impression is created by workmen appearing to carry out one task, leaving the site for a week and then returning to do something else.

CHAPTER 5

Planning and Inspection

The inspection of buildings must be done on an objective basis by a clerk-of-works or inspector with training and considerable experience. The maintenance manager should aim to keep the standards of repair and decoration as uniform as possible for any similar group of buildings since, particularly in estates of houses, users and occupants compare standards avidly and are inclined to suspect favouritism where additional work is done. The difficulty lies partly in the variety of problems that can cause building materials or components to wear or decay. These include climatic conditions, pollution, fungi, insect attack, subsidence and flooding. They seldom attack a group of buildings in a uniform manner, and the lack of uniformity is made worse by the fact that occupants and users treat their buildings with varying degrees of consideration.

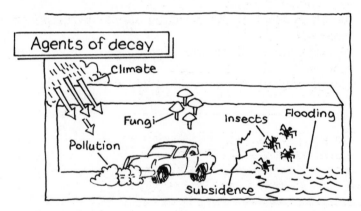

Figure 5.1

Thus the plans and programmes, and the budgets that are calculated from them, cannot be completely rigid, and it will be necessary for the maintenance manager to switch resources and re-allocate funds if an inspection reveals unexpectedly severe deterioration. Therefore, an important part of the maintenance manager's work in planning activities is to work out a systematic

Figure 5.2

approach to the inspection of the buildings for which s/he is responsible. For each building s/he has to provide the answers to six key questions:

1. When should the building be inspected?
2. What should be inspected?
3. What maintenance should be done as a result of the inspection?
4. At which level of deterioration should a component be repaired?
5. At which level of deterioration should a component be replaced?
6. Should preventive maintenance be carried out?

Figure 5.3

The first question should be answered from the maintenance master plan. For any one financial year it is necessary to list the buildings which are due to be inspected, together with any backlog from previous years. The next question, 'what should be inspected?' is more difficult, since so much depends on the judgement of the member of staff carrying out the inspection. However, the problem can be eased by introducing standard forms, report layouts and check-lists, so that the inspector has a ready reference to the details that s/he is expected to gather.

Figure 5.4

Once this system has been introduced, a file can be built up on each property showing the inspection reports and work carried out over a period of years. This will assist in giving guidance on the rate of deterioration of materials and elements, so that the decision on the need to repair or replace any particular item following a five-yearly inspection can be made in a more logical fashion.

Setting up a filing system
Except in the case of small properties, which may be dealt within groups, a separate file should be opened for each main building that is to be maintained. If one is available, a working drawing of the building should be inserted in the file (suitably amended to show any alterations that were undertaken during the construction period). This drawing should be regularly updated to show any additional work, particularly alterations to drainage and services, since a great deal of time can be wasted attempting to find their location on site.

Although it is appreciated that this may be difficult where

buildings have been standing for some years, it is much easier to apply in the case of new buildings, as the maintenance manager will be in a position to insist that *all* the details which s/he may require are supplied.

Figure 5.5

The next paper which should be prepared for each file is a general description of the property or properties which it covers. The details which this should contain are as follows:

1. Address of property (with key plan if necessary).
2. Use of property (for example, house, office, factory).
3. Name of occupier (with address if different).
4. Any special instructions (for example where key can be obtained).
5. Date of construction of main building (and annexes if different).
6. Names of builder and architect.
7. Access (pedestrian and vehicular).
8. General remarks on state of building and expected life.

The general description should be updated from time to time as any of the details alter, such as change of use, new occupier, additional construction works. The remaining information will be compiled in the form of an inspection report, which should be written out by the member of staff who carries out the inspection. It may be convenient to separate major items from general decoration and minor maintenance items, since the latter could be set out on a room by room basis on a standard form.

79

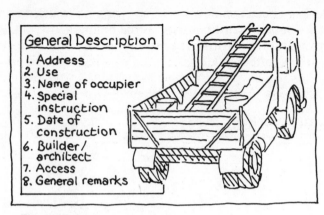

Figure 5.6

A typical standard form for the inspection of individual rooms in a building is shown in Figure 5.8. Although it is not always possible to use standard forms for the internal inspection of buildings, they can usually be applied where a standard design of building has been constructed, such as school classrooms or government houses. In these cases, it is possible to pass a copy of the completed form on to the foreman of the maintenance gang, once the work to be done has been approved, so that s/he will have a clear picture of the workload.

Where the properties to be maintained are of uniform construction, such as government houses on an estate, it may also be possible to devise a form to cover external repairs.

Figure 5.7

Compiling a check-list

Where the buildings are so variable that a standard form cannot be employed, a check-list may be helpful as a reminder to the inspector of the items which s/he should examine and report on. This will naturally vary according to the building types, but the check-list might well take the following form:

Inspection check-list

Roof

Covering	description	*Interior*	access
	finish – main		construction
	– hips		boarded areas
	– ridge		condition of timbers
	– verge		infestation
	other roofs		immediate repairs
	general condition		required
	immediate repairs		estimated life of
	required		main structure
	estimated life	*Rain penetration*	
Eaves	construction	*Insulation*	
	projection	*Storage tank*	material
	defects		capacity
	repairs required		age
Gutters	materials		support
	size		cover
	condition		conditions
	defects		whether replace-
	repairs/redecoration		ment needed
	required		estimated life
Rainwater pipes	materials	*Pipe-work*	material
	size		condition/leaks
	condition		whether repairs or
	defects		replacements
	repairs/redecoration		needed
	required		estimated life
Flashings	chimneys	*General remarks*	
	abutments		
	gutters		
	repairs required		

Walls

Materials used

External finish

Condition (note any cracks)

Pointing

Decoration   material used
                condition

Gables

Plinth

Foundations subsoil
               construction
               settlement
               defects

Air-bricks   type
              size
              position
              obstructions
              any action needed

Damp-course material
              obstructions
              height above ground
              level
              height above floor
              level
              continuity
              pointing
              any action needed

General remarks and work to be
  done

Windows   type
            material
            subframe
            sill
            position in rebate
            finish
            condition of putty
            general condition
            glazing
            any replacements
             needed
            work to be done

External   type
doors   material
            frame
            threshold
            finish
            condition of putty
            general condition
            any replacements
             needed
            work to be done

Flashings   materials
            position
            adequacy
            work to be done

Balconies and
verandahs   construction
            rail
            finish
            any replacements
             needed
            work to be done

Floors

Construction

Stability

Finish

Any infestation

Other defects or damage

Surface condition

Expansion joints

Access traps

Any replacements needed

Work to be done

Staircases

Construction	*Treads* finish
Stability	nosing
Finish	condition
Any infestation	*Rails*
Other defects or damage	*Any replacements needed*
	Work to be done

Internal finishes

Plaster	ceiling	*Fittings*	
	walls	*Decorations*	materials
	finish		standard
	work to be done		condition
Woodwork	condition		work to be done
	any infestation		
	decorative repair		
	work to be done		

Water service

Main supply	position	*Cold-water*	
	type	*service*	material
Rising main	material		condition
	position		repairs or action
	condition		needed
	repairs or action	*Hot-water*	
	needed	*service*	storage
			material
			condition
			immersion heater
			repairs or action
			needed

Electricity service
Report from specialist, if necessary

Drainage

Outfall	foul	*Manholes*	construction
	stormwater		covers
Interceptor			rendering
Fresh-air inlet			channels
			benching

83

Drains	material size condition (state if water, air or smoke tests carried out) any work to be done	*Septic tanks*	size capacity condition outfall work to be done
Waste-pipes	material size condition replacements		
Cesspools	size capacity condition overflow work to be done		

Outbuildings

Description

Condition

Work to be done

Grounds and gardens

Driveways	*Hedges*
Paths	*Trees*
Lawns	*Work to be done*
Gardens	

Boundaries

Fences	material condition work to be done	*Gates*	material condition work to be done
Walls	material condition work to be done	*Unmarked boundaries*	marking to be done.

General remarks

The check-list above would be issued as a general reminder to inspectors, and it would not be necessary for them to report in full on every item for each building in turn. It has been made deliberately comprehensive so that nothing should be forgotten, but the inspector would use his or her judgement in deciding

84

which items should be closely examined and where a cursory examination would be sufficient.

Wherever possible, the general check-list leading to a written report should be superseded or supplemented by a more detailed check-list form with gaps which could be filled in by the inspector as s/he undertakes inspection. It may be difficult to do this where buildings are very diverse in their nature, but could be very helpful for standardized structures such as schoolrooms. In such cases, it will usually be possible to employ a standard layout for decoration and minor repairs to rooms, such as the one shown in Figure 5.8.

Building Inspection Checklist – Internal						
Room name/No.	First inspection		Final inspection			
Item	Surface	Position	Installation	Operation	General	
Floor skirtings						
Walls screens						
Ceiling						
Windows fittings						
Doors fittings						
Fixtures fittings						
Electricity lights and sockets						
Water supply						
Drainage						

Figure 5.8

CHAPTER 6

Organizing Maintenance through Direct Labour

The nature of an activity should always determine the way in which it is organized. A contractor specializing in building repair and maintenance work will approach the problem in a way different to a public sector organization which can plan its work on the basis of a known work load. In addition, the contractor has to give a good deal of attention to obtaining enquiries for work and submitting tenders and estimates, while the direct labour organization will normally only carry out repairs and maintenance to the stock of houses and buildings for which it is responsible.

In either case the schedule of work to be done will be based on an inspection of the buildings to be maintained, which will lead to a list of work to be done on each particular building. Although the budget should give a realistic estimate of the resources required to provide a suitable service on an annual basis, the maintenance manager will have to direct and manage the resources from day to day and week to week to ensure that the actual work needed as revealed by the inspection is carried out as cheaply, rapidly and effectively as possible. The three key resources which must be brought to the right place at the right time are labour, materials, and tools, plant and equipment.

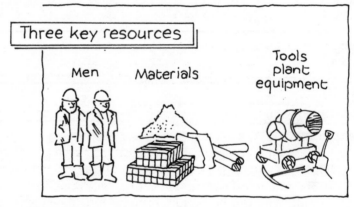

Figure 6.1

Labour

It is certain that the service provided by any building department cannot be better than the quality of the labour-force
employed. This is even truer of building maintenance than it is
of general construction, since craftsmen work in smaller groups
and it is not possible to give strict and continuous supervision.
Thus it is vital that these people should fully understand the
objectives of their work, and be motivated to carry out their
tasks skilfully and effectively. If their only interest is the size of
their pay packets at the end of the day, week or month, they will
be unlikely to provide an acceptable service, and the reputation
of the maintenance department will suffer.

Thus the maintenance manager must be an understanding
manager of men as well as a technically qualified professional.
The intensity of supervision will depend on the number of staff
employed on each building at any one time. On a large
renovation job requiring a substantial labour-force, it may be
possible to run the work like a typical building contract, with a
full-time foreman. On a slightly smaller job there will probably
be a working foreman or charge-hand. However, many of the
smaller jobs will not even justify this degree of supervision and a
group of two or three workers would probably be instructed and
supervised by a travelling supervisor, with responsibility for a
number of jobs.

One way of improving the performance of the work-force,
particularly where it is only possible to provide occasional
supervision, is to introduce some form of financial incentive
scheme based on a measurement of the work carried out.
Targets can be set for individuals, although this tends to take

Figure 6.2

time and be expensive, so it is often better to set targets for a group of workers doing the same job. The setting of targets is an important activity and must be done on the basis of considerable knowledge and experience of general building work, as the targets must be acceptable as fair and reasonable by the employees, while ensuring improved performance.

If the targets are too low and easily reached, there will be no incentive to work more effectively and output will not improve as it should to cover the cost of increased wages resulting from the bonus payments. On the other hand, if targets are set too high, the operatives will find that they have no hope of reaching them and the incentive effect will be lost.

Figure 6.3

Once the bonus targets have been set, they should be kept at the same level for a reasonable period. If an employer is suspected of raising bonus targets 'because the men are earning too much money', they will slow down their output and make jobs appear more difficult than they really are. This can be done more easily on repair and maintenance work than on major construction contracts, since supervision cannot be so close. It is even more vital to earn the loyalty of employees by fair treatment.

A bonus scheme should not be seen as an alternative to proper supervision, because it can only work if there is good supervision. But it is a way for a good employer to share the benefits that result from a fully motivated performance with the operatives that contribute to better standards and a higher volume of work.

There is a number of ways in which incentive schemes can be

operated. The crudest method is simply to subcontract the labour element in the work at a fixed price for each part of the job, or according to a schedule of rates. This has the advantage of enabling the employer to know precisely the labour cost that will be involved before the job is started, but also the severe disadvantage that the labour-force is unlikely to feel much loyalty towards the employer as they have no expectation of continuing and improving working conditions.

A better way to provide an incentive scheme is to employ workers directly at a generally accepted wage rate, and pay a bonus related to productivity once their output has passed a target figure. It is important that the target figure for bonus purposes is known and understood by the labour-force in advance, so that they can appreciate the required level of output and to avoid unnecessary arguments about bonus levels after the work has been done.

Figure 6.4

Of course, bonus schemes are no substitute for good management. If a workman does not have the right tools or has to wait for detailed instructions or materials do not arrive when they are needed, s/he will be unable to reach the required output but will not be blameworthy. In fact, if s/he fails to earn a bonus due to mistakes made by management, s/he will feel that s/he has been cheated. Thus, incentive schemes must go hand in hand with improvements in management. It is only by a combination of incentives with good management that a bonus scheme can effectively raise the level of productivity.

There is, of course, much more to managing a labour-force than providing instructions, wages and financial incentives. It is

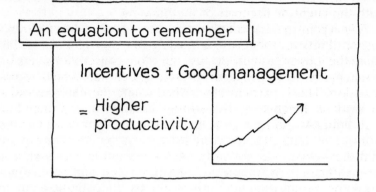

Figure 6.5

also vital to ensure that the workers are properly trained to do the work expected of them. Building maintenance involves a great variety of tasks, and it is unlikely that new recruits will be fully experienced in all of them.

Since they will be required to work in small groups and show initiative in dealing with problems as they arise, proper training for building maintenance workers should be seen as an investment in tools, equipment and other physical assets. If the organization and its work-load is large enough, it will be well wothwhile organizing special courses, which can be tailor-made to suit special requirements.

These courses should not be limited to craft skills, but should also cover the other special skills that will be needed if the maintenance activity is to be properly organized and controlled. They would include recognition of faults and appropriate repair techniques, unit costs of common repair items and recording and measuring completed work.

Supervisors should be chosen carefully, as it is always difficult to find sufficient workers with a suitable blend of skill, knowledge and experience who can be trusted to represent faithfully the interests of their employer. Although the foreman should certainly be experienced in the trades that s/he is required to supervise, technical knowledge alone is not enough. There is also a need for human skills and a strong personality so that the workers for whom s/he is responsible respond by giving of their best.

It is also vital that the supervisor should be trusted and backed up by the employer. S/he should have the freedom to make decisions within his or her own area of responsibility, such as

90

ordering plant and materials and discussing day to day problems with the client or occupier of the building.

A final point in this section must be the vital one of the employer's responsibility for the health and safety of employees. Partly because the jobs are usually of short duration, concern for safety on maintenance work appears to be less in evidence than on new construction. This is particularly marked where there is a necessity to work at heights, as the cost of erecting and dismantling scaffolding would be high in relation to the overall cost of the work to be done. It is the responsibility of the employer to see that the workers do not run unnecessary risks. Although it is often difficult to provide for standards of safety and welfare that would be required on new constructions, the employer should see that they do not fall below a minimum acceptable standard.

Materials
The cost of building materials, particularly those items which have to be imported, rises year by year and accounts for a high proportion of maintenance expenditure. Once s/he has ensured that the labour-force is well-managed, the main potential savings open to a maintenance manager must come from better purchasing and a more economic use of building materials.

The first step must be to review purchasing and storage arrangements to ensure that the appropriate items can be supplied rapidly when they are required. In many cases it will be important to ensure that new materials match closely with the old, so a greater variety of items will have to be stocked than for new construction and a good stock-recording system must be put into operation.

Figure 6.6

A maintenance manager is subjected to many more pressures than an executive responsible for new construction. For new buildings there is usually an agreed completion date and a programme of work is drawn up to ensure that it will be met, so, providing the construction work on the site proceeds according to the rate set out in the programme, s/he knows that the client will be satisfied. However, the person who is responsible for the maintenance of buildings once they have been constructed will often, despite a programme of preventive maintenance, be faced with emergency requests to deal with immediate problems. S/he will naturally want to deal with problems as promptly as possible, so the main anxiety will be to get labour and materials to the job without delay. Thus it is easy to overlook the need to review purchasing procedures in order to ensure that the cost of materials is brought down to a minimum figure. The five basic objectives in purchasing are to buy:

the right quality
at the right time
from the right source
in the right quantity
at the right price.

The first consideration is naturally to see that the quality of the goods provided conforms to the requirements, which may be that new bricks match with existing brick buildings or that a special window frame should be made up to replace one that has rotted or decayed. It is not enough just to order goods of the correct quality. It is also necessary to ensure that the foreman or site representative inspects the goods carefully after they have

Figure 6.7

been delivered to make certain that they conform to the order and to the requirements for the work.

The second consideration must be to ensure that the materials are delivered to the job at the right time. Late delivery of materials is a very common cause of low productivity, as the operatives and craftsmen cannot be blamed for failing to get on with their work when they have no materials to work with. All receipts of materials should be entered in a 'goods received' book or standard form so that invoices can be checked later. The foreman should be instructed to report any additional or outstanding items so that the supplier can be asked to deliver them in time to be incorporated in the work.

Figure 6.8

The source of building materials for maintenance jobs can be either from stock or from a materials supplier. Although there are great advantages in keeping a good inventory of stores including the opportunity to make bulk purchases at good levels of discount, care must be taken in selecting types of material for stock. Where there are good records of past work, it should be possible to estimate reasonably accurately the quantities of standard materials such as cement, concrete blocks, timber and paint. However, holding stocks itself costs money. Although it is convenient to be able to draw any particular item from one's own store rather than to have to wait for delivery, it is also important to calculate the best level of stocks to provide a useful service without tying up too much capital. Apart from the risk of items being stolen, getting out of date, deterioration or being destroyed by fire, the storeroom itself is an overhead, and one that can only be charged to the stocks held. So, the longer an item is held in stock the greater the additional overhead charge that it attracts, and this may easily be greater than the inflation in the prices of equivalent new materials.

Attention must also be given to ensuring that the correct quantity of each item is delivered for each job, including a reasonable allowance for breakage or wastage where this is appropriate. It is foolish to hold up a carpenter due to shortage of nails or screws, but it is also important to keep track of these small items as they can cause a significant increase in costs if they are made available without check.

The fifth consideration is to buy at the right price. The 'right price' may not always be the lowest price, since the right price is the price which leads to the lowest cost of a material when it is ready to be installed. A reliable supplier who quotes a standard price may well be preferable to one who is less reliable but offers some form of discount to attract business, and the alternative quotations must be carefully evaluated.

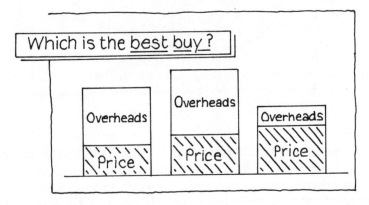

Figure 6.9

Among the on-cost factors which must be taken into account when deciding the addition to the price that will give the true cost of the item are:

1. Purchasing overheads including office costs.
2. Costs due to defective materials.
3. Costs of carrying stocks.
4. Losses if work is disrupted.
5. Costs of double-handling materials.
6. Costs of poor service by supplier.

94

Figure 6.10

It is easy to calculate precisely the varying contributions to on-cost resulting from dealing with a series of different suppliers, but it is certainly possible to make a subjective judgement as to which of the suppliers gives a prompt and reliable service. In fact, where there is a good supplier in the district, it is less important for the maintenance department itself to hold a high level of stocks. In this case, a slightly higher unit cost can be absorbed by savings on costs of carrying stocks, of double stocks and of double-handling materials.

Another general point is that the larger the order placed with a supplier, the keener s/he will be to obtain the business with the result that the unit prices should be lower. So, it can pay to calculate the annual requirements for timber, cement, iron-mongery, paint, and so on, and ask for competitive quotations on the basis that the goods should be delivered at a fixed price month by month over the whole period.

Tools, plant and equipment

A maintenance department is not likely to require as large a budget for plant and equipment in relation to turnover as an organization specializing in new construction work. Since a maintenance department usually has to deal with a large number of fairly small jobs rather than a few large ones, the need is for a variety of small tools and light equipment that can be transported easily and used for a wide variety of work.

The sort of work that a typical estate maintenance department would be called upon to carry out would include external painting, as well as repairing defective window sills and frames, repairing loose door-frames, new eaves, gutters or down-pipes and repairs to broken or defective doors. There will also be a need for repairs to plumbing, drainage and sanitary work and there may be a call to undertake bricklaying, blocklaying and plastering work. Many building maintenance departments also execute electrical repairs and maintenance.

The stock of tools, plant and equipment to be held as a matter of policy will have to be decided on the basis of the prevailing type of activity in which the maintenance department is involved, as well as the types of building for which the department bears responsibility. The stocks will consist of three main types of goods:

Plant. Major items such as benches, ladders and trestles which should last for many years.

Tools and equipment. Small tools such as hammers, chisels, drills and trowels.

Stores. Minor items that will be needed to carry out repair work from day to day, such as screws, nails, hinges and locks.

As a guide to the types of plant, tools and equipment and stores which might be required for various types of work, the following tables have been prepared, although these must naturally be reviewed and modified according to local requirements:

Plant	Tools and equipment	Stores
Plumber's bench	Blow lamp	Solder
Jaw vice	Mallets	Taps
Pipe vice	Hammers	Waste traps
Taps and dies	Chisels	Ball valves
Pipe rocks	Scrapes	Guttering
	Files	Rainwater downpipes
	Plungers	Drain-pipes
	Drain rods	C.I. pipes
		Manhole covers
		Inspection pit covers
		Basins
		Sinks
		Baths
		Sanitary-ware
		Putty
		Paint

Figure 6.11 *Typical items required for plumbing and drainage work*

Plant	Tools and equipment	Stores
Ladders, various lengths	Paintbrushes, various	Paints
Step ladders	Putty knives	Varnish
Trestles	Scissors	Glasspaper
Scaffold boards	Scrapes	Steelwork
Dust sheets	Screwdrivers	Paint cleaner
Tarpaulins	Pincers	
	Pliers	
	Glass-cutting bench	
	Diamond for glass cutting	

Figure 6.12 *Typical items required for painting and decorating*

Plant	Tools and equipment	Stores
Scaffolding	Large trowels	Cement
Ladders	Pointing trowels	Sand
Trestles	Floating trowels	Lime
Scaffold brackets	Hammers	Plaster
Scaffold boards	Chisels	Tiles, various
Mortar boards	Rule	Drain-pipes
Buckets	Screwdrivers	Half channels
Hods	Shovels	Step irons
Wheelbarrows	Plumb bob and line	
Plaster boards	Straight-edges	
	Scrapes	

Figure 6.13 *Typical items required for bricklaying, blocklaying and plastering*

Plant	Tools and equipment	Stores
Bench	Pliers	Light bulbs
Ladders	Screwdrivers	Cable, various
Scaffolding	Chisels	Conduit, various
Testing apparatus	Hammers	Switches, fitments
	Drills	Clips
	Torch	Fuse wire

Figure 6.14 *Typical items required for electrical repairs and maintenance*

97

Plant	Tools and equipment	Stores
Joiner's bench	Handsaws, rip	Files
Clamps	Handsaws, cross-cut	Ironmongery
Vice	Handsaws, panel	Nails
Extending ladder	Handsaws, tenon	Screws
Step ladders	Handsaws, dovetail	Door furniture
Scaffold boards	Chisels	Window furniture
Drill	Gouges	Cupboard furniture
	Screwdrivers	Hacksaw blades
	Hammers	Paint
	Mallet	Varnish
	Paintbrushes	
	Hacksaw frame	

Figure 6.15 *Typical items required for joinery and general repairs*

Administration

The effectiveness of a maintenance department must depend on the skill of the manager in applying the three key resources of labour, material and equipment. Good clerical and administrative procedures can make a very valuable cotribution to ensuring that the department provides an appropriate level of service to the users and occupiers of buildings as well as increasing the economic life of the capital assets that the buildings represent.

In turn this implies that a prime task for the maintenance manager is to steadily build up a filing system of management information upon which s/he can base decisions. Whilst the procedures that should be followed in a particular department must depend upon the administrative needs, certain basic forms will certainly be required as a matter of course.

As outlined in chapter four, three basic forms which should be prepared for medium-sized and major maintenance jobs are a daily labour allocation sheet showing the number of workers in each gang employed on various tasks, a materials sheet detailing the materials employed in each job, and a job sheet describing the work carried out and detailing any additional expenses. Examples of each of these forms which provide the basic information for a costing system are shown in Figures 6.16, 6.17 and 6.18 on the following pages.

Inspection reports and working drawings should be filed according to the property to which they refer. It will normally be best to keep separate files for each building although in some

Daily Labour Allocation

Job no.   *Address:*

Gang: *Foreman/Charge-hand:*   *Date:*

Task									Total hours per person
Name	No.								
Hours per task									

Figure 6.16 *Typical daily labour allocation sheet*

Materials Sheet

Job no.   Address:

Gang: Foreman/Charge-hand: Date:

Description	Make	Catalogue no.	Size	Received at job		Returned to store	
				Quantity	Value	Quantity	Value

Figure 6.17 *Typical materials sheet*

100

```
┌─────────────────────────────────────────────────┐
│                   Job Sheet                     │
│                                                 │
│      Job no.                    Address:        │
│                                                 │
│                                                 │
│   Gang:          Foreman/Charge-hand:    Date:  │
│                                                 │
│                                                 │
│   Work carried out:                             │
│                                                 │
│                                                 │
│   Extra work or variations:                     │
│                                                 │
│                                                 │
│   Date started:                                 │
│   Date finished:                                │
│                                                 │
│   Additional expenses:                          │
│                                                 │
│                                                 │
└─────────────────────────────────────────────────┘
```

Figure 6.18 *Typical job sheet*

cases files may cover a group of buildings. Other forms and written records should cover:

1. Staff and employees: personal records, wage or salary rates, records of training.
2. Pricing records: for maintenance of up to date price records of materials.
3. Purchase orders: for materials, plant and equipment.
4. Receipt forms: for payments received.
5. Maintenance record forms: for use in planned maintenance.
6. Wages sheets: for preparation of wages.
7. Petty-cash forms: to record minor cash payments.
8. Maintenance request forms: to be sent in by occupier to request repairs.
9. Job cards: authorizing work given to foreman or charge hand.

Typical forms for all these activities have not been specified since needs vary greatly from one organization to another, and suitable forms should be designed by the maintenance manager after a careful analysis of his own procedures and needs. The steps to be taken are as follows:

1. Check all existing forms. Do they provide all the information required? Do they give any information that is *NOT* needed?
2. Redesign existing or design new forms as necessary.
3. Check the sequence of operations, and re-arrange as necessary.
4. Check the number of operations and reduce as possible.
5. Decide who should deal with each operation.
6. Check to see that the procedures provide the information required in time for the right decisions to be made.

It will then be necessary to ensure that all staff and employees understand what is expected of them, and review the procedures after a period to check that they are working out as expected. It may also be helpful to issue a short manual to building occupiers so that they will understand the maintenance services that are available to help them, and will hopefully take a more positive interest in ensuring that the buildings which they occupy are properly looked after.

CHAPTER 7

Organizing Maintenance through Contractors

Some organizations prefer to employ their own labour to maintain the buildings for which they are responsible, while others prefer to use contractors for this purpose. The use of contractors is most common for major projects which occur when buildings have to be demolished and replaced. There is, however, an established trend toward the use of contractors for rectification and repair, and specialist firms are now also offering their services for the more mundane tasks of cleaning and servicing.

From the point of view of the owner, there are certain advantages to be gained from the use of contractors. The main advantage is the transfer of risk, management and employment responsibilities to the shoulders of the contractor. Another factor is that contractors are frequently able to achieve higher levels of output and productivity than direct labour-forces. On the other hand, a well-organized direct labour-force offers the owner a degree of flexibility and control that is not available once dependence on contractors is established.

It should be noted that maintenance contracts do not have to refer to specific physical tasks, as laid out in bills of quantities for new buildings. It is quite feasible to let annual maintenance contracts based on indicative requirements, with remuneration based on a schedule of agreed rates for labour, materials, equipment and overheads. Indeed, it is also possible to let contracts for cleaning and servicing in which the contractor agrees to keep facilities to an established standard of upkeep in return for a negotiated fixed annual sum.

Kenya: a case study
Rather than offer general advice on the execution of maintenance works through contractors, the view offered here is based on the conditions in Kenya. This is mainly because contractual frameworks are somewhat diverse, and hopefully it will be more helpful for the reader to relate his or her own conditions to one specific country rather than be given a string of generalizations.

Registration of contractors

The Ministry of Works in Kenya maintains a register of approved contractors. The register contains a list of all contracting firms authorized by the Ministry to carry out the construction of new projects and maintenance works throughout the country. The process of registration is centralized but the list is distributed to all district offices. The register is maintained to ensure that only competent contractors are engaged to carry out construction or maintenance works whether for the government or private organizations. All public institutions such as central government, local authorities and parastatal organizations use this list when considering contractors for the award of tenders. Private institutions and individuals also only deal with approved contractors registered by the Ministry.

Any firm wishing to be registered must complete an application form and submit it to the Ministry of Works' headquarters through the branch office. The contractors will then be classified by type of work (electrical, plumbing or general construction), complexity of work, value of work and status. The Ministry can refuse to register an applicant for lack of qualifications or equipment.

A firm may be downgraded if it ceases to fulfil the conditions of registration or if it proves unsatisfactory in its contract relations or otherwise forfeits the confidence of clients and consultants, particularly in the execution of public projects. Equally, it is possible for a contractor to apply to be upgraded on the grounds of greater experience and/or increased financial and physical resources.

Invitation to tender

In Kenya, as in many countries, the annual maintenance cycle is closely aligned with the financial year of the organization concerned. This is particularly pronounced in the public sector. Thus, at the beginning of a new financial year, the maintenance officer in a particular district or province picks out various jobs deferred from the previous year together with priority jobs for the new year and carries out a detailed inspection of the buildings in question. The maintenance surveyor then prepares the necessary specifications and tender documents.

S/he may either invite public tenders in the press or (as often happens) suggest a selected tender list from the register of contractors. The contractors to be invited to bid are selected on the basis of estimated cost, together with the complexity and location of the work. Normally the list contains at least 12 names. The selected contractors are invited to collect the tenders from the contracts office or they are posted to them. A locked box in which tenderers must place their tenders is fixed in a prominent place in the contracts office. The tenders are opened at a particular time and all tenderers are free to attend or be represented at the formal opening of tenders.

Selection of contractor
After opening, tenders are examined to ensure that the prices are reasonable and that the bids do not contain serious errors or omissions. The tenders are examined against the materials and labour rates prepared by the Ministry of Works cost planning unit. These rates are based on analyses of construction costs on previous contracts. The general practice is that if the lowest tender is found to be unusually low, the department will write to the contractor asking for the tender figure to be either withdrawn or confirmed. Besides the tender sum, the completion time offered by the contractors is compared against the estimate.

Competitive tendering
The submission of the lowest tender does not automatically indicate that the contractor submitting that tender is the most efficient of those tendering. A low tender may be the result of inaccurate estimating or of a shortage of work in the locality, or it may be set deliberately low with the intention of cutting the quality of workmanship. Yet public projects are usually awarded to the lowest bidder. Too frequently, however, the outcome is that the administration of the contract becomes difficult, and time and cost overruns can occur when contracts have to be terminated and new contractors appointed. In general, the results from selected tendering are better than those from open tendering, since there is an opportunity to weed out firms with a bad reputation or inadequate resources.

Negotiated contracts
A negotiated contract is one for which the contract amount is determined by a process of negotiation, rather than on the basis of sealed bids. In Kenya, one reason for the use of negotiated contracts is that the government is endeavouring to encourage the development of an indigenous construction industry, and negotiation is limited to local firms. A contract may be negotiated directly with a firm owned by indigenous Kenyans

for values of less than about US$6,250. All jobs above this value are let through competitive tenders.

Negotiation is not merely a way of helping a local construction industry; it also permits the greater involvement of the contractor during the design process and perhaps encourages speedier completion and better-quality work. Indeed, negotiated contracts are quite common where repair and redecoration works are required in lease-expired premises. For such tenders, the department and the contractor determine the tender amount based on standard rates prepared by the Ministry of Works. Negotiated contracts are quite common for specialized works such as plumbing, electrical work, roofing or underpinning of walls for which there may only be a limited range of specialists. They are also useful for general rehabilitation and repair contracts, where it is difficult to foresee the scope and complexity of the work until the problem areas are exposed and inspected. For the client, negotiated contracts can offer real advantages, providing negotiations are limited to competent contractors of proven integrity.

Contract administration

Contract documents are prepared by the maintenance department and include:

1. Articles of agreement signed by both parties.
2. Conditions of contract appropriate to the work being carried out, with or without bills of quantities or for minor works.
3. Priced bills of quantities or a specification signed by both parties.
4. A Surety Bond signed by the surety (for contracts over US$6,250).
5. The form of tender submitted by the contractor.
6. A copy of the letter of acceptance signed by the maintenance department.

Site supervision

Supervision will be handled by a building, electrical or mechanical inspector depending on the nature of the contract. The supervisor's responsibilities cover:

Site organization and management
1. Including ensuring that the contractor employs a competent site foreman

Contract documentation
1. Check that copies of the general specification, bills of quantities and particular specifications (if applicable) are available on site

106

2. Study the contract documents and report any apparent errors, omissions, discrepancies and ambiguities to the contracts officer
3. Keep accurate records of authorized provisional items, omissions and additional work

Quality of workmanship and materials
1. Examine all workmanship and materials
2. Draw the contractor's attention to any shortcomings and, if they are not rectified, report this to the contracts officer

Site instructions
1. Prepare and sign site instructions covering variations in the work or specific instructions to the contractor. In Kenya, site instructions must be countersigned by the contracts officer before being issued to the contractor
2. Where a site instruction will give rise to a change in the cost of the works, an estimate of this change must be made and recorded before the contract officer's approval to issue the same is requested
3. All site instructions involving a variation in the cost or duration of contract should be covered immediately by a variation order which is the only document which can legally vary the terms of a contract.

The supervisor is expected to keep a site diary and submit weekly reports to the maintenance surveyor to enable him to evaluate the progress of the job. If the contractor is entitled to an interim payment, the weekly site report may be used to estimate the payment due, although certificates are normally based on measurements by a quantity surveyor on all but the smallest jobs. When the supervisor is satisfied that the contractor has completed the specified work, s/he prepares the certificate of practical completion which will be countersigned by the mainten-ance department before the final payment can be prepared.

Defects liability period
After the certificate of practical completion has been issued, half of the ten per cent retention money is released to the contractor. However, a five per cent retention sum is retained during a six-month defects liability period and is only released after a certificate has been issued confirming that all defects have been made good.

Damages
Liquidated and ascertained damages may be applied to the contractor who fails to complete the works by the set completion

date. The damages are calculated according to the daily or weekly liquidation damages specified in the contract for the period during which the works remain incomplete, that is the time between the contract completion date and date of practical completion. Damages for non-completion can only be applied after due notice in writing has been given to the contractor, and may be waived if the contractor is able to show that completion was delayed for extraneous reasons. Examples could be inclement weather, or a delay in the issue of variation orders, or additional work having been ordered after the contract was signed. Damages may be deducted from an interim payment, although such settlements are generally delayed until the final certificate is issued.

Determination of contract
Contract conditions allow for the employment of a contractor to be determined by the employer. Grounds for this include default, bankruptcy of the contractor and wrongful assignment. It is recognized, however, that determination of a contract is a serious step to take and the repercussions are time-consuming and expensive. It is often preferable to advise and assist the contractor to complete the works without determination. Where a contract is determined, the contractor is usually downgraded or struck off the register of approved contractors.

Maintenance of essential services
Special provision is required to minimize or avoid downtime of essential services. Accordingly, the maintenance department keeps a register of mechanical plant, and the department's inspection team survey major items every three months. As the equipment is inspected, comments on the condition of the component and when it is due for replacement are included in the remarks column of the inspection chart. The inspection team, which includes artisans as well as technicians, is equipped with basic tools to enable them to attend to minor repairs.

On receiving the completed chart from the inspection team, the maintenance department will decide on further action. If the repairs to be carried out seem uneconomical (say more than half the replacement cost) the client ministry will be informed accordingly and requested to provide funds for a replacement.

At the beginning of each financial year the maintenance department receives one half of the total allocation of funds for each essential service being maintained by departmental labour. The balance is paid after six months. If a repair costs under about US$2,500 the department will authorize the work to be carried out as a minor maintenance job, and charge the cost of the work to the appropriate minor maintenance works' account.

If a repair costs more than US$2,500 the maintenance department must arrange for the work to be done by contract labour. Sometimes, if the work is urgent other items on the works programme can be deferred to provide the necessary funds. Generally, the jobs to be deferred are low priority jobs whose postponement for a few months would not adversely affect the operation of the plant as a whole. However, the department may have to use minor maintenance funds to keep the plant going during the period of postponment. Although the contract procedure is essentially the same as previously described, special care is taken to select only competent and reliable contractors, so that downtime of essential services is minimized.

PART THREE
METHODS

CHAPTER 8

The Influence of Design

A section on building maintenance problems and their solutions must start with a chapter on the influence of design. Although the designer should be part of the solution, all too often s/he is part of the problem. Admittedly, it is hardly possible to design a building that would be completely maintenance-free. Its cost would approach that of a spacecraft, entry to it would have to be severely restricted, and its users would probably find it uncomfortable and unfit for its purpose. But it *is* feasible to design a building for minimum maintenance, and it is sensible for designers to examine concepts such as cost in use and to look carefully at the trade-off between initial cost and maintenance cost. Indeed, there are many occasions where a shrewd and experienced designer can even evade the trade-off by designing a building which is both economic in the first instance and relatively cheap to maintain.

Two ways
There are two ways to make a building cheap to maintain. The first is to make a deliberate effort to minimize defects during design and construction, and the second is to detail and choose materials and components in such a way that the job of the maintenance manager and the maintenance gang is made less onerous and difficult. What can be done about it? To start with, wise clients will open a line of communication between their designers and their maintenance managers. They will also ensure that maintenance records are prepared in such a way that they highlight avoidable costs. Too often maintenance records are like historic balance sheets and profit-and-loss accounts; they tell the manager where the money has gone – but too late to do anything about it!

Good maintenance records will enable managers to pin-point designs, materials (and designers and contractors) which lead to persistent trouble. If Pareto's law holds good, 20 per cent of each of these will give rise to 80 per cent of the trouble in its category. The next step is to check whether there is a reason to give the offender a second chance. If not, the client should take the final step of avoiding the particular design, material, designer or contractor on future jobs. The scope for savings through this simple procedure could be immense.

Design defects

The UK Committee on Building Maintenance[1] suggested four main reasons for the existence of design defects in buildings:

1. Inadequacy of the client brief; the architect as a professional is expected to assist the client in developing an adequate brief.
2. Inadequacies of design; most design errors are errors of specification, or choice of materials, juxtaposition of incompatible materials or components, and inadequate provision of safe access for maintenance.
3. Construction errors, due to ambiguity or inadequacy of specification or supervision.
4. Defects in materials and components.

These reasons stem, in the main, from the direct actions or omissions of the designer, and are responsible for 20 per cent of the annual cost of repairs in the United Kingdom.

Total building maintenance

If the above estimate of 20 per cent is generally applicable, by inference the remaining 80 per cent of the cost of repairs must be attributed to the normal wear and tear of the building fabric. At first sight normal wear and tear is inevitable, by definition, and the designer may expect to be absolved from any responsibility for these costs. However, while there is a limit to the extent to which the designer can forecast – much less control – the use of a building, this should not overshadow the fact that the designer cannot really escape responsibility for maintenance whether regular or abnormal as s/he has rationalized the future outlook of the building.

Furthermore, it is not always easy to draw a distinction between the cause of a defect and normal wear and tear. For instance, it is not technical detailing alone that may cause rapid deterioration of the buildings when compared to the effect of density or intensity of use; or aspects of space requirements. These aspects may be attributed to conceptual design rather than draughtsmanship or detailing. It is often assumed that errors in detailing arise because the designer leaves the details of

1. *Report of the Committee on Building Maintenance*, op cit.

113

his or her vision to be worked out by draughtsmen who are technically unqualified, and may arrive at solutions which turn out to be unsatisfactory. Although this is a possible source of maintenance problems, good detailing is an integral part of good design and the designer should check working drawings carefully before they are issued so that faults are identified and corrected before the construction phase.

The rate of deterioration
When the buildings are in use, the rate of deterioration is affected by climate, user activities and changing tastes and habits. The extent to which these agencies cause deterioration and thus create a need for remedial treatment will depend on the adequacy of the design and the suitability of materials specified, the standard of workmanship in the initial construction and subsequent maintenance and the extent to which the designer has anticipated future needs. The first and the last factors are of particular interest because they are often ignored or treated lightly in current literature in favour of technical detailing.

Future needs
It is the future needs that will affect size, layout and services, and these may, in the long run, have a great bearing on the need to maintain or modernize buildings. In the case of one local authority in Kenya, of the 3,398 tenancies no less than 68 per cent of the family units were accommodated in one- or two-roomed apartments. Large families are the rule rather than the exception in Kenya, resulting in occupancy rates of 4.7 persons per room. The consequences of this design decision are that social problems may result from too many people living together; equally there is the question of increased maintenance costs and the shorter life of buildings and facilities due to intensive use and abuse. Small units also cost more to maintain in terms of plumbing and redecoration when compared to larger units. This underlies the need to appreciate the role of socio-cultural factors in building design, and to take realistic account of probable occupancy rates. Admittedly this is easier said than done, in view of the pressure to make limited housing budgets go as far as possible in providing additional accommodation. However, it is a useful principle to design for maximum flexibility and provide for possible extensions. An example is core plots on site and service estates, which allow for additional rooms to be built when funds are available, whereas apartment blocks can only be extended or modernized at considerable expense.

114

Design and maintenance: a case study
How design affects maintenance can be illustrated using a case in which the performance of flat roofs was compared with that of pitched roofs. Roofs are the most difficult structural element of a simple building, and there are several reasons why they may be expensive or require frequent maintenance. This will depend partly on whether they are flat or pitched, and partly on how well they are designed and constructed once the choice has been made. The case described is based on the Kenya study referred to earlier.[2]

'Flat roofs
Unusual rainfall. Most flat roofs tend to pond when water is not drained away as quickly as forecast, leading to leakage, particularly around drainage outlets. The study noted that Mombasa has a mean annual rainfall of 1,182 mm with 46 as the mean number of rainy days in a year. Precipitation is generally highest in the month of May when the mean rainfall is about 235 mm. However, in 1982 Mombasa had a rainfall of 1,672 mm, of which 664 mm fell in 23 days of the month of May alone. Therefore in 1982 the rainfall was higher than the average by 61 per cent, and for May alone the rainfall was more than twice the average amount. Given that the size of the outlet allowed for the normal flow of rainfall per hour was based on the records for the past 44 years, the rainfall for the year 1982 could not be easily drained. The ponding was aggravated where the design did not provide for a proper fall, which should be more than 1 in 80.

Debris. Ponding may also be caused by blockage of the drainage system due to the presence of debris or tree leaves or birds nesting. Here is a case where regular minor, and wholly labour-intensive maintenance to clear away such deposits can yield major savings. Although materials like asphalt or bitumen are impermeable, persistent ponding at the same place causes a gradual deterioration of the bitumen felt. Where ponding has caused roof leakage, it may be necessary to relay the roof or provide a new covering over the whole area. This can be very expensive.

Gradual deterioration. Sometimes the covering material such as asphalt or bitumen may begin to deteriorate. For instance, during hot weather, asphalt becomes relatively soft and may blister due to vapour pressure of water trapped in the concrete underneath. Also, if the base on which asphalt is laid begins to move through expansion or contraction, the asphalt may crack. This would be particularly common in Mombasa where solar heat gain is high. The designer should therefore consider minimizing solar heat gain or allowing for expansion and contraction through provision of expansion joints.

2. P.M. Syagga, 'Impact on Building Design on Maintenance costs' Ph.D. Thesis (Nairobi 1985). (Summarized in Appendix 1)

Both blistering and cracking effects on asphalt also apply to bitumen arising from water vapour or roof movement.

Pitched roofs

Sagging structure. Pitched roofs have the tendency to sag or spread. The structural timbers may have become bowed due to long-term loading, beetle attack or corrosion of nails and other forms of fixing. Sagging roofs may be supported using struts, or be wholly replaced.

Deterioration in covering. Covering materials for pitched roofs such as galvanised corrugated iron sheets may rust, asbestos cement sheets may crack, while tiles may slip. Buildings bordering or close to the sea are particularly vulnerable. For example, Mombasa lies on a longitude 4° 02'S and latitude 39° 37'E, bordering the Indian Ocean. It therefore has high temperatures and humidity which tends to accelerate the corrosion of iron sheets. There is therefore need to paint the sheets to reduce or delay the rate of corrosion.'

The results of the study in Mombasa showed that the roof repairs cost 20 per cent of the total fabric maintenance cost, as against 29 per cent for plumbing and 25 per cent for decoration. Flat roofs tended to cost more per house than pitched roofs, being 1.49 times the cost of pitched roofs. This points to the fact that the provision of flat roofs in the tropics is a hazardous proposition. The Government of Kenya has, in fact, subsequently issued a circular to the effect that no public buildings should be designed with flat roofs in the future in view of observed failures in institutional buildings such as hospitals, schools and residential blocks of flats.[3]

Faulty choice of materials

Other aspects of design failures have to do with choice and the location of building materials under given climatic conditions. In a hot and humid tropical climate, exposed steel pipes on wall surfaces are subjected to atmospheric corrosion. The metal is attacked by dampness in the air, sometimes assisted by pollutants, and this leads to rusting and premature failure.

Leakage

Besides corrosion, another common defect on external as well as internal pipework is leakage at the joints resulting in dampness affecting the walls. The following are some of the reasons why leaks may occur at joints, and there may be more than one reason for any one defect:

3. The Standard correspondent, 'No more flat roofs', *The Standard Newspaper* (Nairobi 1986).

116

1. Thermal expansion and contraction under extreme climates. When expansion is restricted, particularly at the joint, plastic materials with a high coefficient of thermal expansion are more vulnerable to joint failure. Contraction, on the other hand, results in the pulling out of compression joints.
2. The joints may leak as a result of bimetallic corrosion occurring when dissimilar metals such as copper and steel have been jointed.
3. Chemical action of fluxes, for instance, used in making joints may cause the pipe to become perforated; the joint may also leak because it was improperly made originally.

Decoration

Decoration, which includes painting internal as well as external surfaces, may be subject to defects intrinsic to a particular material or defects arising from incompatibility of the finish and its background. The most common defect on paintwork that calls for frequent decoration of both external and internal surfaces is discoloration, which can result in fading or discoloured patches. One possible cause of this defect is dampness, resulting from rain penetration or condensation. There is also the possibility of chemical action from the alkali formed by the interaction of lime and alkali salts in any moisture which may be present. This may change the colour of pigment used in the paints. Discoloration is common in areas where buildings do not have roof overhangs to shelter walls.

The external surfaces of buildings also become dirty over time, depending on the capacity of the surfaces to retain the dirt that falls on them. All external air contains particles of dirt and greasy material, and staining is facilitated during periods of heavy rain. The incidence will be most pronounced in buildings fronting main roads and those near industrial areas. Thus, brightly painted colours on buildings with flat roofs look very attractive for a few months, but end up requiring redecoration after every period of long rains. Either the walls should not be painted at all, or they should be painted in dark colours. Better still the roofs should be pitched in the first place.

The role of the designer

An important part of the role of the designer is to enable creative solutions latent in and conceived by the client or community to emerge. Such a designer, while becoming closely identified with the goals and objectives of those for whom s/he works, retains the distinction of having powerful specialist tools

117

and techniques at his or her command. These relate to the imaginative expression of latent solutions, simulation, and prediction of consequences in terms of technology and resources. In essence, the designer should be able to predict the ultimate effects of a proposed design scheme on users and the society as a whole, so that the ultimate work gives both satisfaction and value for money. S/he should be aware of good or bad effects of alternative designs upon issues which are important to the users but which may not be of direct financial interest to the developer. The tendency of many designers is to consider only the interest of who pays the fees as the 'only client', particularly in cases of housing developments for sale. The consequences of such an attitude can be disastrous to owner-occupiers in later years, and will ultimately rebound on the reputations of both client and designer.

The need for feedback
Such is the separation of roles in the construction industry that designers mostly are not, and never have been, builders. Thus the designer may specify a product which is not readily available, or which may be both difficult and expensive to assemble on site. There is a considerable advantage to be gained if it is possible to involve the builder right from the beginning when design work is in progress. Sometimes this can be achieved directly through some form of 'package deal'. At the very least there should be a feedback of information on performance in use from previous projects. The design should no longer be the work of one person on the drawing-board starting with a plain sheet of paper. There is need to involve many people including designers, developers and users or maintainers, so as to take into account the complexities and inter-dependencies of social, economic and technical considerations.

It is not being suggested, however, that the role of the designer as a professional should be surrendered to self-help through public participation by all those who have an interest in buildings. The central issue according to J.F.C. Turner (see Chapter 1), is that of control or 'who decides'? The role of the public is to set performance standards, that is, setting limits to what practitioners may do. This is not an unreasonable proposition, because it is the users who know what they need most, and are therefore in the best position to choose in a given situation. Once the choices are made, they have to be translated into a buildable form by the designer using his special nature training and skill. Figure 8.1 illustrates the cyclic nature of the

118

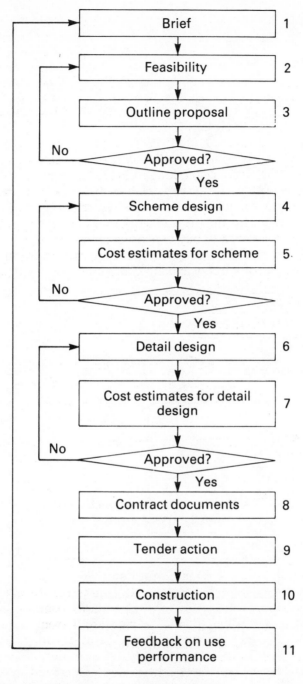

Figure 8.1 *Cyclic nature of design process*

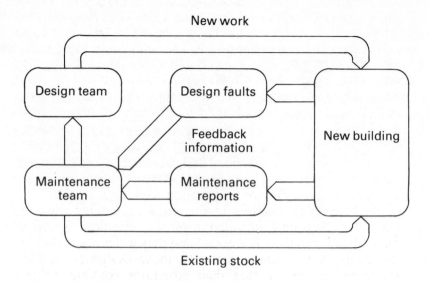

Figure 8.2 *Feedback cycle*

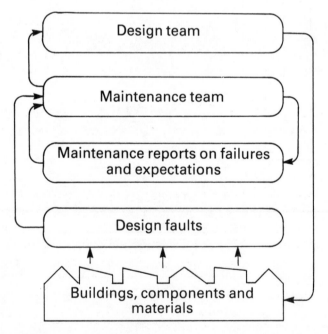

Figure 8.3 *Flow of feedback*

design process, and it is evident that feedback on use of performance (which is essentially the outcome of the analysis of maintenance data) is the last stage in the design loop. If this is ignored by the construction industry, then the likely cost of maintenance will not be known, and hence the total life-cycle cost of a building cannot be determined. The potential lessons to be learned from comparisons of value for money of alternative designs will therefore be lost.

The designer *needs* the participation of users and maintenance managers to obtain effective feedback; they must be regarded as an integral part of the extended design team. Figures 8.2 and 8.3 show the importance of the feedback cycle in the construction industry, and the flow of information within it.

The remaining chapters of this book offer hints, tips and general background information on the technical aspects of building maintenance. It is hoped that they will be useful both to the maintenance manager and to those designers who are concerned to ensure that their structures continue to give satisfaction to both owners and users over their full design lives.

CHAPTER 9

Building Structure

Foundations

The most expensive repair bills in building are often due to foundation failures of various kinds, as fundamental defects in the construction of foundations are almost always very expensive to correct. Where foundations are built on rock, there is little chance of failure, providing the rock is sound and solid. But most buildings have to be built on soil, which is enormously variable in its bearing capacity and can be generally defined to include all deposits of loose material.

As long as foundations are properly designed to suit the site and the characteristics of the subsoil, the building constructed upon them should last a long time, perhaps even hundreds of years. It must be accepted that all buildings which are constructed on soil rather than rock are bound to settle to some extent. The fact that the soil is bound to be disturbed when the foundation trenches are dug and compacted, together with the increased loading due to the construction of the building on the land must lead to at least a small amount of settlement as the subsoil reacts to the superimposed load.

Where the settlement is uniform over the whole area of the building, it is unlikely to cause any damage and will not be noticed by the occupiers. Damage to buildings is usually the result of what is known as 'differential settlement' in which one part of a building subsides more than another, leading to cracks, stresses and strains in the superstructure.

Wherever possible, differential settlement should be avoided by good design. Firstly, the architect should check that ground conditions are uniform over the whole area that the building will occupy. Secondly, s/he should aim to ensure that the building design is such that the ground will be reasonably evenly loaded and that the foundations are deep enough and substantial enough in relation to the bearing capacity of the subsoil. It is usually best to have strip foundations running under all the walls, and if they are sufficiently deep there should be little settlement in most soils.

122

Figure 9.1

However there are certain types of soil, such as shrinkable clays or the expansive soils encountered in many areas of the central part of the Sudan (often known as 'black-cotton soils'), which require special precautions. Buildings erected on conventional strip foundations on soils such as these almost invariably develop unsightly cracks, and in some cases the structural stability of the building may be endangered (Figure 9.2).

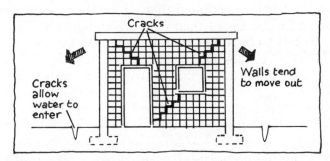

Figure 9.2

In these cases, it is sometimes necessary to resort to a much more expensive slab or raft foundation, in which the building is constructed on a reinforced concrete slab to ensure that the whole foundation acts together in resisting stresses in a similar way to a raft floating on the sea. It must be remembered that the slab will be somewhat flexible, so that some movements can be transmitted to the superstructure, causing cracking in rigid masonry walls. Thus, it is advisable to provide a number of construction joints in the walls to take account of this problem.

Another form of foundation construction which has been used successfully in difficult ground conditions in single-storey houses in India and Kenya is the hard-core platform. In this

123

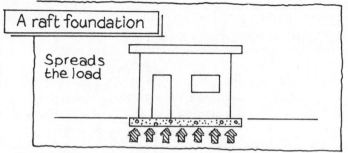

Figure 9.3

method the house is designed to stand on a raised platform of hard-core which stands on a cushion of granular material laid on the black-cotton soil formation. The hard-core is laid to a compacted depth of approximately 40 cm, and the sloping sides of the hard-core platform are grouted with a sand/cement mixture to keep them firm. The hard-core is then covered with a thin layer of sandy gravel and a concrete slab with steel-mesh reinforcement about 10 cm thick is laid on top (Figure 9.4).

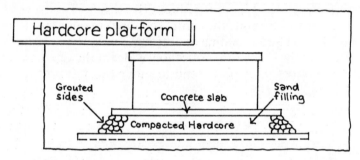

Figure 9.4

Another possibility, although it is usually considerably more expensive, is to design the whole building as a solid reinforced concrete box strong enough to move as one body if the soil should move. In this method, the foundation, walls and roof form a solid frame consisting of reinforced concrete columns and beams infilled with good quality bricks or blocks set in cement mortar.

The surest form of foundation to resist ground movement is one that is sufficiently deep to penetrate below the zone where volume change takes place, so that the building effectively rests on a more solid and unchanging formation. This is achieved by

124

either driving piles into the ground or by digging down or boring out a hole to the formation level and casting the piers in place or building them up in blocks or bricks to just below floor level, where they are capped with a reinforced concrete beam which carries the walls.

Although these specialized types of foundation are inevitably more expensive than a conventional strip foundation, their use is justified in difficult ground conditions since repairs to foundations after they have failed are likely to be even more expensive. When there are signs of differential settlement of the foundations, such as severe cracking, the first step must be to identify the cause so that the inspector can determine whether the settlement is likely to continue and become more serious.

Cracking in the walls is the obvious sign that some form of differential settlement has occurred. The position and type of the cracking provides a clue to the area of the foundation that has settled, as well as suggesting the reason for the failure. It is important to remember that cracking can also be the result of some form of inherent defect in the walls themselves, and this possibility should be considered by the inspector.

There are two main ways in which differential settlement can affect a structure. Figure 9.5 shows the result of settlement at the ends of a wall, while the centre section remains at its original level due to a lighter loading or a stronger underlying soil. It will be seen that the cracks are noticeably wider at the top than at the bottom, as the outer parts tend to move away from the more stable centre section.

Figure 9.5

The other most common type of damage due to differential settlement in a single structure is illustrated in Figure 9.6, with narrow cracks at the top widening as they run downwards. This is caused by the outside parts of the wall remaining firm while

125

settlement occurs under the centre section. Of course the pattern of cracks may be made more complex if the wall contains windows and doors.

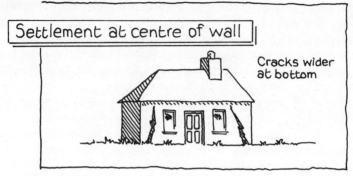

Figure 9.6

Buildings with additions are more likely to suffer damage from differential settlement than single structures, since the loading in the added part will probably be different, the type of construction may be different and the foundations may have been taken down to a different level. It is also possible that the foundations of the main building may have been damaged during the construction of the addition. Although the bonding-in of additional brickwork to existing brickwork helps, it is not sufficient to resist any substantial stresses caused by differential settlement.

Figure 9.7

In foundation repairs, particularly, it is vital to be quite sure of the nature of the defect and the likely success of the remedy before any work is done. Alterations or repairs to the found-ation work of an existing structure are almost always difficult and expensive and time and effort spent on careful initial

126

inspection is well worthwhile. The first thing to check is that there is no immediate danger of collapse. If there is, the building should be evacuated. If not, it will probably pay to wait until the settlement is completed before taking action, so that alternative remedies can be carefully considered.

If the foundations have not been properly recorded on plans and drawings, it will be necessary to dig a series of trial pits to determine their size, type of construction and condition. On a large structure, it will be necessary to undertake a full soil survey, but a useful soil investigation can be made by examining the various strata for certain basic characteristics:

1. Type of soil.
2. Whether it is uniform.
3. Whether it is breakable between the fingers.
4. Whether it is gritty, smooth, plastic or sticky.
5. Whether any plants or organic matter are present.
6. Colour and smell.
7. Depth of ground water.

It should be possible to define the cause of the failure reasonably accurately. There are five main causes:

Overloading of foundations

Overloading can be caused by a number of different circumstances. Firstly, it is possible that the building is being used for a different purpose than that for which it was designed. A dwelling-house for example may be used as an office with heavy

Figure 9.8

127

overloading may have resulted from a bad original design or from some alteration to the building after it had been erected. An example would be the enlargement or insertion of a window filing cabinets and office equipment, or a shed may be used as a factory or warehouse. However, it is also possible that the or door, leading to the transfer of a load to an adjacent section of wall and increased stress on a particular section of the foundation. Thus, it is as important to ensure that a competent architect or designer is responsible for structural alterations to existing buildings as it is for new work.

Consolidation of soil below foundations
Where there is no alternative to constructing buildings on difficult ground, the result is the heavy settlement of structures with conventional foundations. Soils with a high silt content or large amounts of organic matter are liable to settle, and this is also likely when a building is constructed on made-up ground.

Undermining of foundations
Flooding, underground streams or even leaky drains can cause strip foundations to be undermined. In addition, the foundations of an existing building can be seriously damaged by excavations to a new construction. Direct damage can result from the loss of support from one side of the foundation, which can lead to the wall above bulging out on the unsupported side, or else by water flowing from under the existing foundation into a new, deeper excavation, carrying finer particles with it, leading to compaction and loss of support.

Soil movement under foundations
Damage can easily be caused to foundations in clay soils when the clay expands during the rainy season and later shrinks when it dries out. This effect can be made more serious if there are large trees nearby, since their root systems can penetrate the area occupied by the building. A further possible hazard can occur when buildings are constructed on sloping ground, as clay soil has a tendency to creep downhill gradually leading to strains and stresses on the foundation. The remedies that can be carried out to deal with each of these five categories of failure are analysed below:

Overloading of foundations (Remedy)
The cheapest way to deal with this problem is the obvious one of relieving the overloading. Another possibility may be to redistribute the load more evenly so that no particular part of the foundation is subjected to extra heavy loading.

A more expensive solution, which would be justified for

128

valuable and expensive buildings, would be to 'underpin' the existing foundation. This is done by shoring or propping up the existing building, digging down below the existing foundation in short sections and concreting a more solid foundation around it (Figure 9.9).

Figure 9.9

This work must be carried out by an experienced group of direct labour workmen or entrusted to a reputable contractor, since the stability and safety of the whole structure can easily be endangered. Excavations under the existing wall must be carried out in short sections, and should be done in a pattern such that the new foundations will steadily take over from the old in accordance with a sequence such as that illustrated in Figure 9.10.

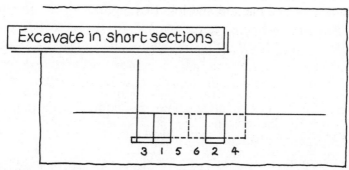

Figure 9.10

Consolidation of soil below foundations (Remedy)
If serious settlement occurs under the whole building, it may be necessary to construct a ground beam running under all the walls to even out the load. However, if it occurs at one corner it may be sufficient to dig down and support that point with a brick, block or reinforced concrete pier.

129

Undermining of foundations (Remedy)
If it is suspected that damage may have been caused by leaky drains, the first step should be to check for leaks by means of an air or water test. If the test shows that the drains are leaking, they should be repaired or renewed, which should at least prevent further settlement. However, if the drains are not completely renewed it will be necessary to check them regularly for a further period to ensure that no further leaks occur. The next stage may to be provide concrete ground beams or to underpin the lengths of wall which have settled.

If the damage has been caused by new excavations to a greater depth than the old foundations, then the existing foundation will probably have to be supported by underpinning or other means. In addition, if a new building is to be constructed very close to an existing structure, the combined loading of the two buildings may be sufficient to overstress the subsoil, leading to a need to strengthen the foundations of the existing building.

Soil movement under foundations (Remedy)
If the movements in the building are due to the action of tree roots and the trees have not reached maturity, the first step should be to cut down the trees close to the building and poison the roots with sodium chlorate or another suitable weedkiller. However, if the trees are mature it is possible that more damage would be done by cutting them down.

Floors
Floors of houses and other buildings do not normally have to stand up to flexural stresses and strains, but they do have to withstand loads and abrasion due to the activities of the occupiers and the furniture and equipment which they use and accumulate. In addition, a crack-resistant and dust-free finish is required to comply with health and hygiene standards, and the floor should be laid reasonably flat and even so that it can be regularly and effectively cleaned. Economy is important, particularly for low-cost housing, and locally-available materials should be used whenever possible.

The floor level should be higher than that of the ground outside to prevent the entry of surface water, and a layer of hard-core or a waterproof membrane is likely to be needed where there is a danger of the floor becoming damp as a result of ground water being drawn up by capillary action.

In short, what is needed is a hardwearing and washable floor surface at a cost which is reasonable in relation to the usage of the building and the funds available. Where the existing floors in an otherwise satisfactory building do not meet the above

130

standards, consideration should be given to replacement or resurfacing to provide a more acceptable living or working environment.

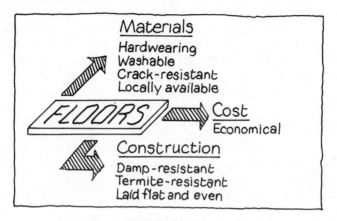

Figure 9.11

The simplest and cheapest flooring material is mud, but mud floors can easily become damp and must be swept regularly and kept dry. Cracks in mud floors should be filled in; and they will occasionally have to be relevelled and replastered. In addition, mud floors have poor resistance to abrasion and are easily penetrated by the sharp edges of heavy furniture or damaged by impact when furniture or equipment is moved around the building.

In many existing low-cost homes, the mud floor has been left at the level of the surrounding ground. These can be improved at virtually no cost by simply raising the floor level about 100 mm by laying and compacting additional earth-fill. A mixture of moist soil and sand might be preferable to ensure maximum compaction. If cement is available, the mud floor can be further improved in terms of strength and durability by the addition of two to ten per cent of cement to the mixture.

A further possible way of improving a mud floor is to lay a thin concrete screed over the mud to provide a better wearing surface. This usually leads to a worthwhile improvement, although thin unreinforced concrete floors tend to crack easily, allowing the penetration of dampness and the intrusion of termites. In addition, rough concrete floors are very difficult to clean as dust and dirt clings and will not be removed by simple brushing. They are also hard on the feet, especially for young children, although this disadvantage can be counteracted by laying mats made from straw or palm leaves.

131

To be really satisfactory, a concrete floor slab should be about 75 mm thick and the finished floor level should be at least 150 mm above the surrounding ground level to avoid moisture penetration. It is normally a good idea to put down a layer of hard-core (stones or broken bricks) under the concrete slab, to help prevent moisture. A thin layer of sand or ash 'binding' should be laid over the hard-core to provide a level surface for concreting. In areas where the soil is very stable or there is very little rainfall, costs can be cut by leaving out this layer. In any case, the earth under the floor should be well rammed to make sure that it is sufficiently stable and compact to provide the maximum support for the concrete floor slab.

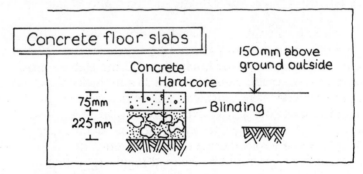

Figure 9.12

Except in very dry areas, it is advisable to lay a damp-proof membrane on top of the blinding layer to prevent further moisture seeping through and making the floor damp. A dry floor is better for slowing down the deterioration of materials in the building, but it is also much more hygienic for the people who occupy it. Polythene sheeting about 0.5 mm thick will make a satisfactory damp-proof membrane, and is not very expensive compared to the overall cost of the floor. It is also worthwhile treating the soil immediately under the floor slab to prevent attack by termites.

Ideally, concrete floors should be strengthened with steel-mesh reinforcement to provide flexural strength and prevent the possibility of cracking, but this decision will depend on the local cost and availability of steel reinforcement and the degree of permanence and quality of construction required.

Concrete for floor slabs must be carefully mixed, and care taken to ensure that the right amount of cement is included in each batch. It is vital to ensure that too much water is not added to the mixture. It is very common for labourers to add a great deal of water to concrete so that it will be 'workable' and easy to lay. They do not realize that the additional water will weaken the concrete permanently, making it prone to cracking and causing future trouble for the building owners and occupiers.

When laying a floor slab in a building, it is best to think out carefully the order in which the concrete should be laid in each room before the work starts. The best place to start is the part of the room which is most difficult to get at and furthest from the door. The mason can then work steadily towards the door so that it will never be necessary to cross over the laid slab. If the work cannot be completed in a single day, a construction joint will be necessary. The mason should arrange for the joint to be made at a doorway, left straight and even and in-line with one side of the door.

It should be possible to trowel the surface of the concrete slab sufficiently smooth to use as a finished surface. But if this is not achieved due to poor workmanship and the slab is left with a rough surface, a sand/cement screed 25 mm thick can be applied to provide a wearing surface. This must be rich in cement content and is thus expensive. It may also crack if it is not properly laid, so it is best to lay the original slab properly in the first place, and avoid the need for a screed.

Concrete floors should be cleaned regularly so that dirt does not become ingrained. Generally, they should be thoroughly washed at least once a week, and it is good practice to clean and scrub them daily. A hard brush should be used to wash the floor, and it is best to clean a small area at a time starting at the farthest corner from the door.

An alternative to a concrete floor is to lay large flat stone slabs, if they are available in the area. These should be fitted together closely and laid on a bed of sand, and mortar can be used to fill in the joints.

Another possibility in areas where suitable clay is available is to employ burnt bricks or tiles as a flooring material. The latter are only satisfactory if accurate flat tiles are produced, and traditional producers often need advice on improved techniques to manufacture satisfactory floor tiles. However, in many areas it would be quite possible to produce good quality low-cost floors with square quarry tiles laid on bare compacted earth.

Walls

In developing countries walls of buildings may be constructed of blocks, bricks or local soil. While modern forms of construction generally use concrete blocks or burnt clay bricks as structural

133

building units, most countries still have a very large housing stock based on some form of earth wall construction. Although earth walls are often regarded as old-fashioned and consequently in need of early replacement, they can provide entirely satisfactory shelter at a comparatively low cost. Although the life of earth buildings would not normally match that of structures built from more permanent material, it can be extended considerably by regular attention to maintenance and prompt repairs when these are needed.

In fact, there are still many earth buildings in use in various parts of the world which were first constructed centuries ago. It is true that they have lasted longest in areas where there is little rain, since continuous rain can cause serious erosion to the walls of an earth house, but well-maintained earth houses can provide valuable shelter for the life and work of millions of people who simply cannot afford to buy expensive manufactured products. In addition, earth houses save on energy and transport, since they make use of a freely available and universal raw material.

Figure 9.13

The repair and maintenance of walls is discussed under three headings; earth walls, brick walls and block walls.

Earth walls
There are five main types of earth houses, and each has rather different properties and maintenance requirements.

1. 'Wattle and daub'. In this method, a vertical framework of posts and poles is first constructed, and then reeds or small branches are woven amongst them to provide a base on to which the reed can be plastered. The basic timber wall structure is rather like a wattle fence and the method completes its name by the way in which a mud plaster is applied or 'daubed' on the basic timber structure. Figure 9.14

134

shows the sort of building that can be constructed by this method with the wattle in place on the right-hand side of the building, and the process of 'daubing' completed on the left-hand side.

Figure 9.14

The method can only be used where there is a sufficient supply of suitable local timber and has the disadvantage that shrinkage cracks often occur, requiring regular maintenance.

2. Adobe. Adobe work is a simple form of earth-block construction, in which the blocks are formed by placing moist soil into boxes to form them into a block shape. The blocks are removed a short time after they have been made and allowed to dry and set for about a month before they are used as building units. A typical size is $40 \times 30 \times 10$ cm, giving a block weight of the order of 20 kg. The blocks are laid in a 'mortar' consisting of a mud similar to that from which the blocks were made.

The advantages of this form of construction are that it is extremely simple, almost wholly labour-intensive and can be carried out by unskilled workers at a low capital outlay. It is, therefore, a method which is well suited for application in self-help schemes, and provided the work is carefully carried out, the walls should be quite strong and weather-resistant in reasonably dry areas.

The disadvantages of adobe blocks are that they look rather rough in comparison with stabilized blocks or concrete blocks and tend to chip easily. They are naturally not as strong or as weather-resistant as burnt bricks or concrete blocks and are rarely satisfactory in areas where the annual rainfall is in excess of about 25 inches. One way of improving the performance of adobe blocks is to mix in some form of stabilizer, such as cement, lime or asphalt. Another possibility is to plaster the walls or cover them with paint or some other form of surface coating. Methods of providing surface coatings are discussed later in the chapter.

3. Rammed earth walls. This is an *in situ* form of construction, in which strong wooden forms are constructed and moist soil is rammed hard between them, making a solid and durable wall. The soil to be used must be carefully selected and identified and the amount of water added must be properly controlled, so that the walls do not shrink or crack after drying.

   The disadvantage of this form of construction is that the wooden framework must be well-made, and in many areas good timber is expensive. If the forms are not set vertically, the wall will look unattractive and may even prove to be unstable. If the work is done sufficiently skilfully, the walls should be very strong and durable and may not need any surface coating. Many owners, however, prefer to plaster or paint the walls to give a better appearance.

4. Compressed earth blocks. These blocks have a considerable advantage over rammed earth and plain adobe construction, since they should be individually as strong as rammed earth walls, but can be made as time is available over a period and then used together to construct the building. Rammed earth blocks are constructed in moulds approximately 30 cm × 30 cm × 20 cm, which can be made from metal or seasoned timber. In order to remove the blocks easily, the mould should be coated with oil every time it is used.

   The mould is first filled about three-quarters full with moist soil and rammed at least fifty times with a tamper such as a heavy flat piece of metal attached to a piece of pipe. The mould is then filled until it overflows and the block is again tamped fifty times. After this the top can be smoothed off with a flat blade, and removed from the mould. It is best to start by making some trial blocks to see whether they shrink or crumble. The strength of blocks can be increased by mixing in small quantities of cement or other admixtures. If the blocks are well made, the final wall should be satisfactory without any surface coating.

5. Cob. A fairly easy method of construction, known as cob, consists of building a wall of balls of stiff mud each about the size of a man's head. The balls are piled up in thick layers to form the wall, and the wall has to be constructed slowly so that the bottom layers harden sufficiently before they have to

bear the weight of the superimposed layers. Although these houses are easy to build and need very few tools and little other equipment, shrinkage cracks are very likely to occur.

Maintenance. Maintenance of earth walls is generally limited to filling cracks and the regular repair or renewal of surface coatings. Surface coatings can be of various types but, providing they are properly mixed and applied, they will enhance the appearance of the building as well as preventing erosion and weathering, thereby substantially increasing its useful life. Various ways of protecting earth walls through the application of surface coatings are discussed later in the book.

Brick walls

Burnt clay bricks are a valuable building material, since they are portable and can be manufactured locally on a small scale, provided that fuel for firing is available. In areas where there is a prolonged or severe rainy season, burnt clay bricks are often preferred to earth walls on the grounds of greater durability and resistance to erosion.

There are two main factors which affect the strength and durability of a burnt clay brick at the manufacturing stage. The first is the suitability of the clay and the second is the method of firing. In most building uses, the compression strength of burnt clay bricks is more than sufficient to take the superimposed loads since, although individual bricks may have much lower strengths than average due to non-uniform firing, the more critical quality is usually durability, and effective resistance to the effects of water penetration and wetting and drying. The bricks which are most likely not to prove sufficiently durable are those which are soft and underburnt, as well as those which have a hard skin over an underburnt interior.

When considering the need for repairs to brickwork, other than surface coating (which is dealt with later in the chapter), the first step is to decide on how extensive the defects are. Where a few bricks only have started to flake, it may be sufficient just to cut them out and replace them with new bricks which match the existing wall as closely as possible. However, it is also important to find out the reason why the failure has occurred. It may be that defective guttering has allowed a constant stream of water to attack a group of bricks, and the cause as well as the effect of the failure should be dealt with.

Another item to check is the pointing of the brickwork, as soft and loose pointing can easily lead to the penetration of water

137

and gradual deterioration of brickwork, as well as making the building less acceptable to the occupier.

If the walls as a whole appear to need attention, the best answer may be to render or plaster them completely.

Block walls

Blocks for building purposes can be made from concrete or from some form of stabilized soil. Block walls are normally rendered or plastered to give extra protection and a more attractive finish, so that maintenance usually consists of checking the state of the rendering and either patching or replacing it when this becomes necessary.

Roofing

The roof of a building plays the most significant part in ensuring a reasonably pleasant living or working environment for those inside it. The roof will be required at various times to keep out the heat of the sun, the cold and the rain. So it must provide a complete watertight cover. It must also be strong and durable enough to stand up to high winds and, in earthquake areas, it should be firmly anchored to the walls, to prevent sudden collapse.

Roofs can take several different forms, depending on the layout of the building, the severity and nature of local climatic conditions and the local availability of suitable building materials. The three most common types are pitched roofs of various kinds, flat roofs and domes and vaulted roofs.

Pitched roofs

The advantage of pitched roofs is that it is easier to make them weather-resistant compared to a flat roof, and it is also more likely that local materials can be used. There are three common forms of pitched roof:

1. 'Lean to' roof. The shed, illustrated in Figure 9.15, is the simplest form of pitched roof and is pitched in one direction only. The roof is held up directly on all four sides, with one parallel wall higher than the other and the side walls shaped to join them. The disadvantage is that this shape tends to produce a wasteful and useless roof space of an awkward shape, as well as walls which are higher and therefore more costly than they would otherwise need to be. For this reason, the use of these roofs is usually limited to buildings where a roof with a fairly flat pitch will be satisfactory. The 'lean-to'

138

roofs are most common in temporary buildings, or additions to existing buildings.

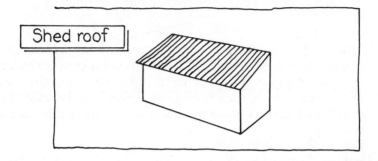

Figure 9.15

2. Gable roofs. A gable roof has a slightly more compli-cated construction, and is shown in Figure 9.16. It has two roof slopes meeting at the centre, or ridge, forming a gable, with the roof covering laid upon a series of trusses. It is a simple, attractive and economical form of construction, with the advantage being that the additional roof space is available in the centre of the building where it is most likely to be useful.

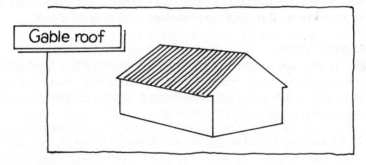

Figure 9.16

3. Hip roofs. The hip roof, illustrated in Figure 9.17, is rather more difficult to build, since, where corrugated sheets or tiles are used, they have to be carefully cut to make the joints. It consists of four slopes all running towards the centre of the building, with rafters at each corner running diagonally to meet a short ridge at the centre.

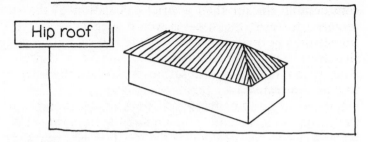

Figure 9.17

Costs and maintenance

The cost of a roof consists of two parts. First, the cost of the roof covering (tiles, corrugated iron and thatch for example) and secondly the supporting structure. In view of the cost of timber for rafters and other support, there is a decided advantage in using a light roof covering where a reasonably durable one is available at a comparable cost.

Typical weights per square metre for common roof coverings are of the order of:

For burnt clay tiles about 40 kg/sq.m
For thatch from 30 to 50 kg/sq.m
For corrugated iron sheets about 10 to 15 kg/sq.m

In addition, tiles weigh rather more when wet (about ten per cent more), and thatch increases in weight to an even greater extent after heavy rain.

Corrugated iron, although it is often a costly imported item, offers considerable advantages in lightness and therefore potential for reducing the strength and therefore the cost of the roof-frame. An additional problem with tiles and thatch is that the roofs should normally be constructed with a steeper pitch than for corrugated iron, to avoid rain being driven under the tiles in windy conditions or gales lifting the thatch. However, where sufficient timber is available to construct a strong roof-frame, tiles and thatch have the great advantage of using local materials.

It is essential that the roofs of structures of all types should be regularly inspected, since a small fault in either the roof covering or the underlying framework can lead to a more serious failure. A point to remember is that the roof structure is the most highly stressed part of a building. The walls, floor and foundations normally only have to resist compressive stress and,

140

for reasons of insulation or durability, walls are normally considerably thicker than a strict calculation of the strength required to resist the stresses would suggest. However, roof frameworks normally have to resist tensile as well as compressive stresses, and the builder must remember that the collapse of a heavy roof could result in serious injuries to the occupants as well as incurring costly repair bills.

Since repair and maintenance work may sometimes require the partial replacement of the underlying framework, it would be best to start by considering the function of a simple pitched roof from first principles.

The simplest possible pitched roof is shown in section in Figure 9.18 below. Although this is very simple and may be successful in small, temporary wooden buildings, the weight of the roof covering together with occasional stresses caused by winds lead to the walls being pushed outwards as shown.

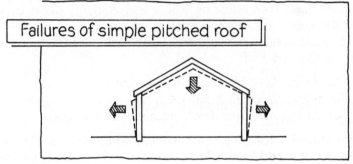

Failures of simple pitched roof

Figure 9.18

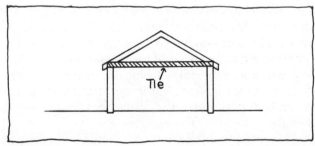

Tie

Figure 9.19

The simplest way to resist this stress is to fix a length of timber to the bottom of the rafters to hold the walls together. The position of this length of wood is shown in Figure 9.19 above,

141

and a series of 'ties' can be sufficient to support roofs which span up to about five metres. An additional advantage of using the ties is that they can be used to hold a ceiling, if this is thought desirable.

With spans in excess of five metres, there is a danger of the rafters sagging under the weight of the roof covering. To prevent this, a pair of struts is inserted joining the centre of the tie beams to the mid-points of the rafters as shown in Figure 9.20.

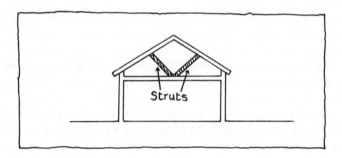

Figure 9.20

A structure of the above type is only likely to be successful up to spans of about seven metres, since the struts push down on the centre of the tie beams, requiring this to be strengthened to carry the load. To achieve this, a vertical piece of wood is inserted at the centre joining the centre of the tie beam to the top of the rafters and forming a complete truss as shown in Figure 9.21. The vertical member is sometimes known as the 'king post' and the truss as a whole as a king post truss.

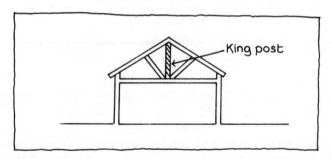

Figure 9.21

142

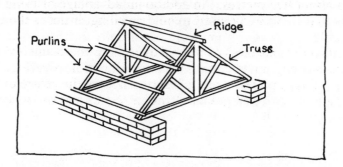

Figure 9.22

It is often easier to fabricate the trusses on the ground, so as to ensure that they are all of exactly the same size, and then lift them up into position so that the actual roofing operation can be completed fairly rapidly. The number of trusses required will naturally vary according to the size of the building and the type of roof covering, but they will normally be set about three to four metres apart.

In order to make a solid framework to which the roof covering can be laid, beams or 'purlins' are attached to the rafters as shown in Figure 9.22 below. The roof covering can then be attached directly to the purlins or, in the case of tiles, a series of battens can be nailed on to support the rows of tiles.

Where verandahs or ancillary rooms are required, these can be covered by simple lean-to roofs as illustrated in Figure 9.23. Besides being more simple to construct, these roofs can also have the advantage of assisting ventilation in the main rooms of the building.

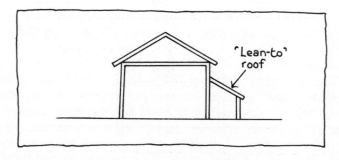

Figure 9.23

143

Repairs and maintenance to timber-frame roofs

Repairs and maintenance to timber-frame roofs of various kinds can be divided into repairs to covering and repairs to the frame itself. Repairs to a framework are usually difficult and can be expensive. The need for repair is usually the result of either some unexpected climatic condition, such as heavy winds or an earthquake, or the steady deterioration of the timber itself. Although good design can minimize the likelihood of a major failure of the first kind, regular maintenance is vital to ensure that the timber does not deteriorate due to rot, fungal or insect attacks.

One of the most serious causes of the deterioration of timber components is a change in moisture content. If a component is made from wood, which has a high moisture content and gradually dries out when it is installed in the building, it will shrink and the joints will tend to become loose. As a result, the structure itself will be weakened.

The second result of a change in moisture content can be a distortion of straight lengths of timber. If the grain of the timber is not straight, the timber components can become warped and lose strength. Where a section of timber is required to withstand a compressive or bending stress, it is more likely to deflect during a change in moisture content than under steady climatic conditions.

Biological attack due to fungi or insects can also be encouraged by frequent changes in moisture content. It is very important that maintenance should be directed at ensuring that timber structural components are properly protected against damp and moisture penetration. This can be partially achieved by protecting the timber by some form of paint or varnish, but it is also vital to see that gutters are free-flowing and unblocked and that the roof-covering itself is kept in a good state of repair.

Thus, although the underlying timber framework should be inspected regularly, it is the roof covering that will be most likely to need regular attention and occasional partial replacement.

Corrugated iron

Although corrugated iron sheets are an expensive imported item for many developing countries, they do have considerable compensating advantages and are consequently quite widely used. They can be transported with relative ease and are quite robust, so they are unlikely to be damaged in handling, loading or unloading or during transit over rough, unmade roads.

Corrugated iron sheets are also comparatively easy to lay and, provided that they are lapped at their sides and ends, should provide a good weatherproof covering. Their useful life is enhanced in hot dry climates, where sheets which are 50 years old and more are still to be found in position in perfectly satisfactory buildings. The sheets are attached to wooden purlins which run horizontally at right angles to the rafters. In order to give a good support, the laps at the end of the sheets should come directly over the purlins; the purlins must be carefully positioned so that this can be achieved as indicated in Figure 9.24. The laps between sheets should be at least 15 cm.

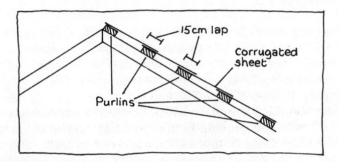

Figure 9.24

The side laps should be at least one and a half corrugations as shown in Figure 9.25 so that the roof will be weatherproof even in conditions of driving rain.

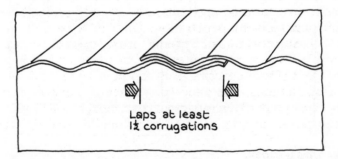

Figure 9.25

Care should be taken to ensure that the individual corrugated sheets are properly lined up and that the joints fit together snugly. If the laps are sufficiently large and the sheets properly laid, the only way in which water can penetrate is through the nail holes. This danger can be reduced by nailing through the

145

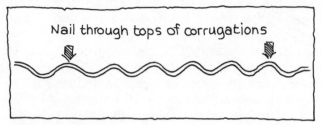

Figure 9.26

top of the corrugations (Figure 9.26) as rain will run in the valleys and any holes in them will always cause leaks.

The nail holes should be started carefully using a thin taper punch so that the sheets will not be damaged and the hole will be no larger than necessary. The nail should be used together with a wider metal washer which will help to spread the stress around the nail hole and provide better resistance to tearing in heavy winds. In addition, a felt washer can be used under the metal washer to take up the slack between the two surfaces and improve waterproofing. The felt washer should be slightly smaller in diameter than the metal one (Figure 9.27). The nails should be driven in firmly to hold the sheets in position but not so far as to distort the sheeting.

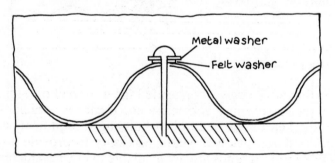

Figure 9.27

The ridge (or top) of the roof must be specially protected to avoid the penetration of rain. It is often helpful to set the sheets a little higher on one side and hammer them over to provide a reasonably weatherproof joint before nailing on the ridging. The three steps required are shown in Figure 9.28.

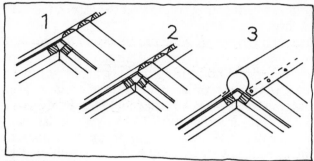
Figure 9.28

The maintenance of corrugated iron sheets will consist of regular inspection, renailing where necessary and occasionally replacing sheets. Where a nail has to be removed, a claw-hammer should be used, and the sheet should be protected with a wooden block as shown in Figure 9.29, so that the stress is spread and surrounding areas of the sheet are not damaged.

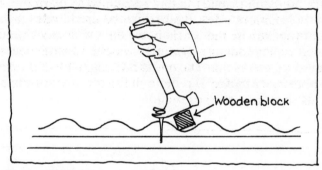
Wooden block

Figure 9.29

A further advantage of corrugated sheets is their potential for re-use after a structure is dismantled. If care is applied when they are taken off the redundant building second-hand sheets can be used and patched where necessary to provide a quite acceptable roof, if funds are not available to buy new materials. Second-hand corrugated iron sheets can also be diverted into a wide variety of non-building uses.

Tiles

If sufficient timber is available to construct a strong framework, tiles can provide a durable and economical roof covering. Where local clays are suitable for tile manufacture, and where enough fuel exists nearby for firing, there is

147

the additional advantage of low costs associated with local manufacture.

A particular advantage which results from the use of tiles as a roof covering is improved thermal insulation. This leads to the buildings being less hot during the day than those with corrugated iron roofs, as well as being rather warmer during cold nights. Many developing countries could profitably examine the potential for promoting local tile-making industries as, in addition to using local materials to produce a satisfactory and economical roof covering, they have the additional effect of generating a significant amount of local employment in rural areas.

Tile manufacture can be carried out on a small-scale basis, providing a suitable clay is available. It is wise, however, to limit small-scale production to simple products that can be manufactured by people with little training and moderate skills using simple and inexpensive tools.

Thus production might be of two general types. Firstly the half round or 'Roman' tile, and secondly the plain or flat tile. The flat tile illustrated in Figure 9.30 has the advantage that the finished roof will be lighter than one built with half-round tiles, with consequent savings on timber in the roof structure. The weight of a plain tile roof covering is likely to be of the order of 70 kg per square metre. It is better if the tiles are not completely flat, but slightly curved in section.

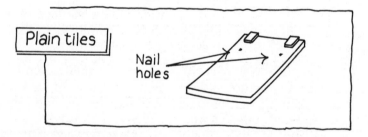

Figure 9.30

The half round or Roman tile (Figure 9.31) results in a heavier roof covering (about 100 kg sq. m.), but may prove more effective in shedding rainwater than a flat-tile roof.

An advantage of using locally manufactured tiles is that when repairs to the roof have to be carried out and tiles must be replaced, similar tiles to the original will be readily available.

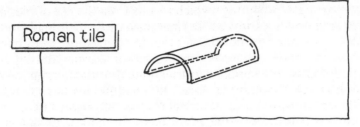

Figure 9.31

However, if tiles are imported or brought from a great distance, replacements may be very difficult to obtain.

Repairs to tiled roofs are not usually too difficult to carry out. Where a plain tile has been broken, it can be replaced quite rapidly by levering up the tile above, taking out the defective tile and sliding the replacement into place with the end nails hooking over the horizontal battens (Figure 9.32).

Where a large area of tiling is damaged, the tiles in the damaged area should all be removed until a surround of sound tiles is left. New tiles should then be inserted, starting from the bottom, and the tiles should be nailed where necessary (normally about every fifth row), finishing with the top row using the method described above for replacing a single tile.

Thatch

Thatched roofs also have the considerable advantage of using local materials and providing worthwhile employment for local labour. If traditional craft skills are available, the thatched roof should not have to be renewed too frequently and may well last

Figure 9.32

149

for 15 to 20 years before needing further attention. There are two major disadvantages which affect thatched roofs. Firstly, they are vulnerable to fire and secondly there is the danger of biological attack or infestation by insects and vermin, particularly in warm, moist climates.

Apart from design considerations which can increase the life of a thatched roof, such as designing it with a steep pitch, additives can be employed to extend its useful life as a covering of a habitable building. Chemicals are available which will retard fire and others will prevent infestation by insects, but these solutions have to be re-applied regularly as they are washed out over a period. The use of bitumen-impregnated string for thatching decreases the chances of insect attack and also protects against rotting of the string.

Where there is a local tradition of thatch construction, it is a particularly suitable material for self-help techniques. The bulk of the cost of a thatched roof is the labour for harvesting, bundling, loading, cleaning, rebundling and the thatching operation itself. Where overall costs of thatched and sheet roofs are comparable, there is a considerable social benefit in encouraging the use of thatch, since it is so labour-intensive and results in the wages element being distributed among a great many local people. A further advantage is that grass for thatching can be transported from the harvesting area in small unit quantities, so that it can be carried on an animal-drawn cart or even on foot, without involving expensive motor transport.

Grass to be used for thatching must be carefully chosen. After the grass has been brought to the building site, it is cleaned and can be combed out so that the individual strands will be lined up within the bundle. A satisfactory comb can be made by hammering a few wire nails into a flat piece of wood. Each bundle of thatch should weigh approximately 15 kg and between three and four bundles will be needed to cover each square metre of roof.

The thatcher should start by laying bundles of thatch at the eaves of the roof and then work up towards the ridge, laying the bundles side by side in rows with each row overlapping the previous one, and tying them to the horizontal battens (Figure 9.33)

Repairs to thatching will normally take the form of renewing the covering at the end of its useful life. However, it is possible to repair small areas by cutting out the original areas and replacing with small bundles of new thatch. After renewal, the area can be raked down and trimmed to match the existing covering.

Figure 9.33

The risk of fire in a thatched building can be much reduced by nailing metal-sheeting under the roof near the fireplace and cooking area. Any cheap second-hand sheeting will do, such as flattened roof sheets, cans or drums. This additional material will cost little or nothing , but could easily save the cost of replacing the whole building and even the lives of the inhabitants.

Fibre-cement products

Fibre-cement (FC) refers to a mixture of natural fibre (sisal, jute, manila or coir), cement and sand, used to make corrugated roofing sheets, single-lap tiles (pantiles), cladding sheets, drainage troughs, and so on. The technology is relatively new, and arose partly from the need to find an acceptable and cheaper alternative to asbestos cement and corrugated iron corrugated sheets. It offers definite advantages in low-cost housing, where it is becoming quite common to combine roofs of corrugated sheets or tiles with walls constructed of soil-cement blocks. The objective of adding fibre to the mortar mix is not to provide permanent reinforcement (as with steel reinforcing bars in reinforced concrete), but to improve manufacturing quality control of the material. The fibre increases the cohesiveness of the wet mix, helping to hold it together while it is being trowelled and shaped; it limits drying shrinkage cracking which occurs as the wet material dries out; it helps improve key strength properties – bending strength and toughness.[1] The sheets or tiles are relatively light in weight, usually being 10mm thick, and are relatively cheap since they have a low cement content.

1. B. Evans, *Understanding natural fibre concrete, its applications as a building material* (Intermediate Technology Publications Ltd, London, 1986).

There is a definite trend towards the use of FC tiles, rather than sheets, for several reasons. Firstly tiles are easier to manufacture, and there is less risk of cracking or breaking due to variations in the mix or inadequate curing. Secondly, they are easier to handle and transport to the site. Thirdly, they can be fixed more easily and with less risk of cracking if there is a lack of rigidity in the roof structure.

The natural fibre concrete technology has been in application for less than 10 years in many developing countries. The average life-span of the materials is therefore not yet known with certainty. It is, however, agreed that fibres in mortar eventually lose strength due to the alkalinity of the mortar, although this is not a serious problem, since it will only occur after the curing process is complete.

Flat Roofs

Reinforced concrete roofs. Reinforced concrete should result in a solid and durable roof, although great care must be taken during construction (particularly curing) because of the danger of the roof cracking and leaking. The roof should be designed by a qualified engineer to ensure that the diameter, spacing and positioning of the reinforcement is correct on the drawings. The contractor should have sufficient experience in working with concrete, and it is important that s/he should be supervised closely by a competent clerk-of-works to ensure that steel-fixing and placing of concrete is correctly carried out.

Jack-arch roofs. Jack-arch roofs are popular in a number of countries in the Middle East, where the local craftsmen are skilled in this form of construction. A section of a typical jack-arch roof is shown in Figure 9.34.

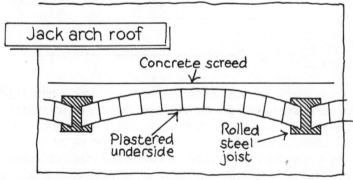

Figure 9.34

152

Jack-arch roofs are generally satisfactory providing they are properly constructed and are particularly suitable in dry areas. However, it is important that the rolled steel joint (RSJ) chosen should be sufficiently strong in relation to the distance which it has to span. If the RSJ is not strong enough, the roof will sag under load and thereby be weakened.

In areas where there is a significant amount of rainfall, the roof should be covered with a weak concrete screed and waterproof covering to shed the rain. The screed should form a slope of at least 1 in 40. Three suitable coverings are:

Two layers of bitumen felt covered with chippings.
Tiles set in bitumen (a good-wearing surface if people are likely   to
sleep on the roof).
Mastic asphalt with chippings.

It is a good idea to ensure that the colour of the upper surface is kept as light as possible, by painting or limewashing, so as to reflect the sun's rays and keep the building as cool as possible.

Pole and earth roofs. A much cheaper form of flat roof, which is still in very common use in hot and dry areas, consists of poles laid side by side, then a layer of matting, topped by a layer of earth about 300 mm thick. The top surface is usually plastered to make the roof surface reasonably waterproof.

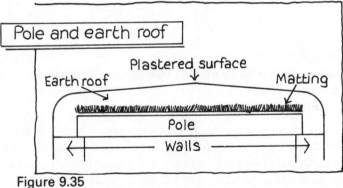

Figure 9.35

These roofs are very cheap and easy to construct, and provide good insulation. However, they are very heavy and special precautions must be taken in areas where earthquakes occur, since collapse would be catastrophic for the occupants.

In areas where rain is likely, there should be a slope of at least 1 in 40 to prevent the water ponding and damaging the roofing materials in periods of wet weather.

Timber preservation

Timber materials and components present their own special maintenance problems which require special attention if they are to be durable and perform well in use. Wood is a versatile building material, and has been used in the provision of shelter in many ways. In areas where it can be easily procured it tends to be widely used, since it is easy to shape on site using fairly simple tools. The trade of carpentry, although skilled, is widely available and understood. Timber has the advantages of light weight, durability and appreciable strength in tension as well as compression. Thus it has a wide range of potential uses in all types of building – for structural framing as well as components, such as door and window frames.

A further advantage in the longer term is that timber is a renewable resource, and it is encouraging that more countries are beginning to appreciate the importance of afforestation programmes, although much remains to be done. Some of the key advantages of timber as a building material are:

1. Its strength-to-weight ratio is good.
2. It is easy to work and structural joints can be fabricated with simple tools.
3. It can be used economically for both load-bearing and non load-bearing requirements.
4. Scrap timber can often be used, making for greater economy.
5. Heavy timber construction is reasonably fire-resistant.
6. It is an attractive and decorative material.
7. The combination of lightness, strength and durability is unique.
8. The material has an appreciable salvage value if the building is demolished.

Unfortunately, there are areas and countries where timber has become unpopular because it can twist or crack in use and is prone to attack by insects or fungi. All building materials eventually deteriorate if they are not properly used, maintained or protected. This can happen quite quickly to components made from wood but, providing the characteristics and maintenance requirements of the material are properly understood and applied, wood can prove to be a long-lasting, pleasing and economic building material. The additional cost involved in treating and using wood properly is comparatively low, and is well-justified by its improved performance and durability. Six main considerations affect the performance of timber components:

Species and type of timber
Felling and sawing
Curing and storage
Usage in the building
Protection
Maintenance

Timber species and types
It is worth remembering that the terms 'hardwood' and 'soft-wood' do not necessarily describe the qualities of the timber itself. In fact it is quite possible for some softwoods to be harder, heavier and more durable than certain hardwoods. Softwoods are timbers from cone-bearing trees, which usually have needle- or scale-like leaves, such as pines. Hardwoods come from broad-leaved trees; these are the most common indigenous timbers in tropical regions. However, there are many different species of hardwoods and they differ greatly in their properties.

Within a single tree, there is a difference between the performance of 'heartwood' and 'sapwood'. When a tree has been cut down, it is often possible to see a difference across the cross-section of the trunk between a darker-coloured centre and the lighter-coloured outer part next to the bark. The sapwood is the living part of the tree, which carries the sap. As the tree grows, new sapwood is formed on the outside year after year producing the distinct 'rings' in the cross-section, while the inner layer 'dies' and becomes heartwood. The structure of the wood is not altered and the strength properties of heartwood and sapwood are much the same in most cases. Hardness, however, which is directly related to the density, may vary. The major difference is in its resistance to insect attack and fungal decay. The heartwood is generally much more resistant, while the sapwood must be treated in some way if it is to perform satisfactorily. Fortunately, it is the sapwood which is the more permeable of the two, so it is therefore more easily and effectively impregnated. In general (although not in all cases, for example, cypress) the heartwoods, which are more resistant to impregnation, are also more resistant to attack.

Since timber grows naturally, as distinct from other building materials which are manufactured under controlled conditions, it usually contains certain natural defects. Thus there is a need for careful inspection prior to use, particularly for load-bearing components. Some common natural defects are:

1. Knots occur where branches once grew in the living tree, reduce the strength of the wood and may lead to distortion during drying. The reason for their formation is that, when

155

the original branches wither away, their bases are enveloped by later growths of annular rings of the main tree. 'Live' knots which are held tight by the surrounding timber are less harmful than loose 'dead' knots.

2. Heart or star-shake occurs if a tree is not felled when it becomes mature, and the movement of resin or moisture causes radial cracks. Where the cracks occur within the heartwood, this is known as heart shake. Where the outside cracks in various places, the cross-section of the trunk resembles a star and the defect is called star shake.

3. Cup and ring-shake are circular cracks separating two adjacent annular rings.

4. Twisted fibres can occur where the prevailing wind consistently turns the tree in one direction, thereby straining the timber fibres.

5. Burls are the result of unsuccesful outgrowths from the trunk of the tree, and can occur if a young tree is damaged.

It is obviously preferable to choose timber that is free from the defects mentioned above, and for structural or decorative use it should be cut from a straight, thick, tree-trunk. The annular rings on the cross-section should be regular, uniform and dense. The colour should be uniform and lustrous. Dark colours often indicate strong timber, and it is a good sign if the timber gives off a clear sound when struck. The timber should be workable, and should not split when penetrated by a nail.

Felling and sawing

After the tree has been felled, the branches are removed, the bark stripped off and the round logs are roughly squared. The next operation is sawing; and at this stage a decision must be made on the way in which the trunk is to be sawn into planks. The choice lies between durable planks (at the cost of high wastage and labour costs) and economical use of the trunk (at the cost of a product which may distort in use). The four main possibilities are ordinary sawing, tangential sawing, radial or rift sawing, quarter sawing:

1. Ordinary sawing is the simplest method, in which the logs are cut in parallel slices by moving the log backwards and forwards in the same position. It minimizes both labour costs and wastage. However, the timber that results is likely to undergo distortion in use due to warping and shrinkage.

2. Tangential sawing, sometimes known as 'plain sawing', consists of sawing planks at a tangent to the annular rings as illustrated in Figure 9.36. Again it is a cheap method involving little wastage, but the timber planks obtained are

156

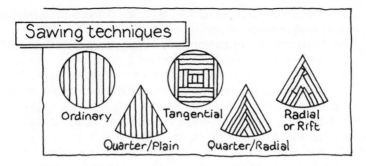

Figure 9.36

relatively weak and may warp during drying and seasoning.
3. Radial or rift sawing. In this method, the wood is cut at right angles to the annular rings, producing timber which is durable and resistant to shrinkage and warping. However, the improved properties must be set against the additional costs resulting from more complicated sawing patterns and wastage.
4. Quarter sawing. This involves cutting the log into quadrants in cross-section, then plain or radial sawing as illustrated. In plain sawing the central portion is effectively radial sawn, while the side portions are weaker. Radial sawing, in this instance, involves shifting the position of the quarter-piece between each saw cut to get the pattern shown in Figure 9.36.

Curing and storage

A living tree contains a large amount of water and freshly converted or 'green' timber may have moisture contents ranging from 40 to 200 per cent of the dry weight depending on the species. Most of this water must be removed before the timber is in a satisfactory condition for building purposes; in general the maximum desirable moisture content for building timber is of the order of 20 per cent. Moisture is present in freshly felled timber in two forms: the cell cavities are filled with water or the cell walls of which the wood is composed are saturated with water.

Wood is a hygroscopic substance and will take up or lose moisture as necessary in an attempt to achieve equilibrium with its surroundings. Thus, much of the initial moisture will leave the timber in any event and, as it does so, the wood itself will swell or shrink to a greater or lesser extent depending on the species. Obviously it is better for the final state of equilibrium to be attained before the timber is shaped and installed in the structure, and this is the reason for giving attention to controlled drying or 'seasoning' of timber. An additional reason for seasoning is that most preservative treatments depend on

157

forcing the preservative into the cells, and it will not penetrate if the cells still contain water.

There are two stages to the seasoning process. First the water in the cell voids moves to the surface of the wood and evaporates. The completion of this stage represents the 'fibre-saturation point', and is usually reached when the remaining moisture content is about 25 to 30 per cent of dry weight. During the second stage it is the water bound up in the actual wood tissue which starts to evaporate. During this stage shrinkage occurs and the timber becomes progressively stronger. The second stage of drying must be carefully controlled, however, or splitting and distortion will occur. There are two main methods of seasoning: air drying and kiln seasoning.

1. Air drying. This consists of piling timber, either in log or sawn form, into stacks in such a way that the free flow of air leads to moisture evaporating steadily from the faces of the timber. The stacking yard should be located on clean, dry and level ground, and the ground surface should be kept free of debris and vegetation so that air currents can move freely under and around the stacked timber. The stacks themselves should be oriented so that air can move through them regardless of wind direction. The timber to be seasoned should be stacked either in open criss-cross layers, or in parallel layers with transverse cross-pieces between layers. Each stack should be put together carefully, with the timber laid evenly so that it will not twist or warp. Five good rules for air drying are:

   (i)   Stacks should be uniform in shape, and preferably under cover.
   (ii) The minimum gap between stacks should be about 1 metre.
   (iii) Timber of different sizes should be in different stacks, wherever possible.
   (iv) Rotten timber should be removed as soon as it is found.
   (v)   The timber should not be exposed to direct sun or rain.

   Air seasoning is cheap and effective, but it is time-consuming and the timber is seldom ready for use in less than six months. Moreover, if moisture contents of less than 20 per cent are required, air drying will not be sufficient and it will be necessary to resort to kiln drying.

2. Kiln seasoning. This is a more expensive method but has the advantages of shortening the drying period and allowing the operator to control the temperature and humidity so as to obtain timber of a desired moisture content. In addition, the artificial heat is likely to kill insects and fungi. Kiln construction

158

and operation is beyond the scope of this volume, but it should be seriously considered in areas where large amounts of indigenous timber are available.

Usage in the building

Many problems can be avoided by ensuring that buildings are properly designed in the first place. Decisions on the general shape of the building will have an important effect on either providing or denying protection to its component parts. Good design can make a cheap and very effective contribution to timber preservation. At the detailed design stage, components and their jointings and fixings need careful consideration to achieve long life with minimum maintenance.

Design is not the subject of this book, but one good example of protection by design is the provision of a large roof overhang. This protects the walls as well as the windows and doors from both rainwater and direct sunlight. The latter can particularly affect timber components, since it leads to high surface temperatures and excessively steep moisture and temperature gradients within the woodwork.

Protection

Sources of decay. Besides climatic factors (moisture, heat, sunlight and erosion), timber is subject to damage by two biological sources. Insects and fungal decay. Of the insects that attack wood, termites are the most destructive, although wood-boring beetles can also cause a great deal of damage in certain areas. There are about 1,900 known species of termites, most of which are found in the tropics. However, for present purposes it is sufficient to split them into two broad classes. These are the 'underground or soil termites' and the 'drywood termites'.

1. Underground or soil termites must have constant access to moist soil with which they can connect by tubes and runways. They can thus be physically excluded from buildings by precautionary measures during the building process and by vigilance on the part of the occupier and maintenance workers. These termites can be prevented from attacking a building by poisoning the soil under and just outside it, or by including some form of mechanical barrier within the structure of the building itself.

2. Drywood termites are usually found in coastal areas and very damp inland areas as they require fairly high relative humidity. They are able to fly and can bore into wood regardless of its location in a building, since they need no contact with the ground. Once established, they form colonies in the wood which they are attacking and are

159

consequently rather difficult to detect. Their presence is indicated by heaps of excreta pellets resembling small light-coloured seeds below the infected timber.

Fumigation is the only reliable method of dealing with drywood termites, and methyl bromide is the favoured agent. Fumigation should be carried out by trained men under proper supervision, and in some areas this may not be possible. Whilst it should kill the existing infestation, it will not confer immunity against reinfestation.

If fumigation is not possible, the best thing to do is to remove and burn all the affected pieces of timber and the pieces near them. This is because it is easy to miss a slight infestation and it is better to burn a little too much timber in the first place them to have to do a major replacement job again later. After removal and replacement of affected timber, the woodwork generally can be brushed or sprayed with a preservative containing a persistent insecticide such as lindane or dieldrin.

3. Powder-post beetles are the most common of the wood-boring beetles. They can also fly into a building or even be carried there in already-infested timber such as furniture or old crates. They attack the sapwood of seasoned hardwoods and reduce it to a fine flour-like powder. Although the damage is limited to sapwood, the beetles may emerge through the adjacent heartwood. In tropical conditions the life-cycle of these insects is completed very quickly. It is quite common for beetles which entered the wood during storage in the timber yard to emerge and re-infect the wood within months of completion of a building, causing serious structural damage within a year to two. In many parts of the tropics where light hardwoods are used structurally, or where the sapwood is included in hardwoods used for joinery and flooring, the risk of attack by powder-post beetles is greater than that of attack by termites.

4. Fungi are plants consisting of microscopic threads which decompose the wood and eventually leave it in a dry friable condition. Other forms of fungi merely cause discoloration, thereby detracting from the appearance of the wood. Fungi cannot grow in dry wood (moisture contents less than 20 per cent), so the most important precaution is to prevent the access of moisture to timber and woodwork. Decay cannot take place in dry wood (although the term 'dry rot' is often confusingly used to describe this process).

Preservatives. The purpose of wood preservation is to increase its resistance to insect attack and fungal action. It also helps to preserve the wood, by making the exterior surface non-hygroscopic, thereby preventing the re-absorption of moisture. To be effective, preservatives must be toxic to kill fungi and insects or inhibit their development. They should also be reasonably permanent. Since timbers which are naturally resistant to termites are very hard and usually expensive and in short supply, some form of artificial preservation is usually required.

There are three main classes of chemical preservative: creosotes, water-soluble salts and organic chemicals.

1. Creosotes are distillates of coal tar and form some of the most important and useful wood preservatives. They are black oily liquids and although they naturally penetrate timber to a certain extent, special methods of application are necessary to ensure full impregnation. Creosotes are particularly valuable for use in exposed situations such as foundation timbers, sills, joints, girders and floorboards embedded in or resting on concrete or in contact with the ground. Their main advantages are:

   (i)   High toxicity to wood-destroying organisms.
   (ii) Relative insolubility in water and low volatility making treatment reasonably permanent.
   (iii) Ease of application.
   (iv) Ease in determining depth of penetration.
   (v)   Oily nature retards moisture changes and provides protection against weathering.
   (vi) Ready availability at low cost.

   Four disadvantages which must be remembered are:

   (i)   Freshly creosoted timber is easily ignited. (When it has dried this problem is much reduced.)
   (ii) It has a powerful and unpleasant smell and food should not be exposed to it.
   (iii) It will soil clothing if spilt, and may burn the skin.
   (iv) Its colour is not attractive for a finished surface and wood treated with creosote cannot be satisfactorily painted.

The advantages and disadvantages must be weighed up for any particular requirement. Creosote should conform to British Standard BS 144 or equivalent and net retention within the wood should be 16 to 48 kg/m^3 for interior woodword and 48 to 96 kg/m^3 for exterior woodwork.

161

2. Water-soluble salts are toxic in nature but are colourless and odourless and specially suitable if the treated wood is to be painted or polished, However, they are less effective as preservatives. Examples are zinc chloride, mercuric chloride and potassium dichromate. Copper-chrome-arsenate (CCA) is quite suitable, with minimum net dry salt retentions of 5.6 kg/m^3 and 8.0 kg/3^3 for internal and external woodwork respectively. Some of the salts are poisonous and should not be used where they can be reached by children or animals, or near food stores. Some are also corrosive to metals. In most cases it is necessary to redry timber after treatment in aqueous solutions before it is used.

3. Organic chemicals. Napthol and phenol are the most commonly-used organic preservatives. They are best suited for surface treatment, and the treated surfaces can be painted. The colour and paintability of the wood, and to some extent the protective properties of the preservative, are determined by the properties of the solvents used. Light volatile oil solvents such as mineral spirits and kerosene that are nearly colourless and evaporate quickly should leave the wood practically odourless and clean. However, light oil solutions may give less protection than those made with heavier oils. Thus for uses where smell, paintability and colour do not matter, heavier oils would be preferable.

Application of preservatives. There are three main ways of applying preservatives to timber: surface treatment, dipping process and pressure treatment.

1. Surface treatment. This is the least effective, although it is the easiest to carry out. It is likely that the treatment will have to be repeated every two to three years, and it is definitely unsuitable if the timber is likely to be exposed to very damp conditions. The problem is that the preservative cannot penetrate deeply into the timber, so surface treatment is particularly ineffective in combating borer-beetles and termites. Since only a thin layer of wood is treated, all cutting, boring and planing of the timber must be completed before the treatment is commenced.

2. Dipping process. Better penetration is obtained by a dipping process in which the timber to be treated is immersed in a tank of preservative solution. Dipping in hot preservative is generally preferable because the heat helps to evacuate the

wood cells so that more preservative is sucked into them. Great care must be taken in the preservation process, since many chemicals are potentially hazardous unless used in strict conformity with instructions.

Whilst ordinary dipping processes are less effective than pressure treatments, 'hot-and-cold open-tank processing' can be a very useful method in remote areas. The equipment required is fairly simple and the process itself is not complicated. It is important that the moisture content of the wood to be treated should not exceed 25 per cent. Creosote is the preservative ordinarily used, but water solutions, such as zinc chloride, can also be used if the solution is kept at uniform strength.

The treatment involves heating the wood in the preservative in a open tank for several hours, then quickly submerging it in a cold preservative for several more hours. This can be done by transferring the wood from a tank containing hot preservative to one containing a cold solution, or by draining the hot preservative from a single tank and quickly filling it with the cold solution. Alternatively the same result can be achieved more easily (but more slowly) by shutting off the heat and allowing the wood and the hot preservative to cool together.

Simple tanks can be made from 44-gallon oil drums. The timber must be completely immersed in the preservative for the duration of the process, and can be weighted down or wedged to keep it below the surface. The preservative must be heated to 80 to 90°C for at least one to two hours after which it is allowed to cool to 40°C. No part of the timber should be in contact with air during cooling if complete treatment is to be achieved. This is because the creosote is drawn into the timber during the cooling period.

The objective is to obtain as deep a penetration as possible with the minimum amount of creosote. If the penetration is not satisfactory, either the time in the hot or the cold bath should be increased next time. If the penetration is satisfactory but too much oil is absorbed, the time in the cold bath should be shortened. The best combination of treatment times must be found by trial and error since it varies with the species, character and condition of the timber.

3. Pressure treatments are the most effective, although they do require more elaborate equipment and are not suited to small operations. The treatment ensures the deep penetration of preservative into timber leading to its

extended life in use, and there is the additional advantage that the timber can be worked after treatment. Since the process must be carried out as a commercial venture in view of the relatively high capital investment, it is beyond the scope of this book. Vacuum-pressure treatment should, however, receive considerations in areas where local timbers are widely available.

Maintenance

The key to proper timber preservation is regular inspection and maintenance. If decaying wood or damage is discovered early remedial treatment will not be too expensive, but if the damage is more serious or if infestation has already occurred, replacement and reconstruction may have to be carried out at considerable expense. The essential point to remember is that inspections should be carried out thoroughly according to routine procedures.

During regular inspections the surveyor should examine all timber for possible damage, whether or not it is loadbearing. Special attention should be given to parts of the building which are tucked away or hidden and not normally seen by the occupiers from day to day. In roofs every piece of timber should be examined; elsewhere it may only be necessary to make spot-checks by lifting occasional floor boards.

All timber should be examined around toilets, baths and sinks, or where there are signs of water-staining on walls or soil heaped against the outer walls. Plumbing leaks, besides creating conditions for decay, also create locally higher humidity which may encourage attack by wood-boring beetles.

CHAPTER 10

Building Finishes

Plastering and rendering

It is quite common for simple walls of various kinds to be coated with plaster. If the plaster is stabilized with some sort of additive, such as cement, the stability of the structure will be much improved compared to an unstabilized wall, without incurring the greater expense that would be involved in mixing stabilizer into the whole wall structure. Against this, extra labour is involved and the surface must be properly prepared so that the plaster will stick firmly in place. There are three main kinds of plaster which can be applied to walls of various kinds: cement plasters, mud plasters and slurries.

Cement plasters

Cement plasters are the most expensive, but also are the most durable providing they are properly mixed and applied. They can only be usefully applied to walls which are not cracking and which do not contain too much clay, since clay is likely to swell and crack the coating. The sort of mix that is likely to be successful in protecting an earth wall is:

1 part Portland cement
4 to 5 parts clean sand
sufficient water to make a thick mixture
small amount of lime if plaster is too hard to spread

Figure 10.1

If the finished work is to be durable and look attractive, it is vital to keep the materials clean, and to ensure that the cement and lime are stored in dry conditions. If the sand becomes contaminated with leaves or mud, or even ballast or bits of dried cement, it will not stick properly to the walls and the work will soon have to be redone. The constituents of the mixture must be measured out carefully, to make sure that exactly the same mix is used each time. It is best first to thoroughly mix the materials while they are still dry. The water can then be added gradually, and the whole mixture thoroughly mixed again. The mixture must then be used as quickly as possible, since it will begin to lose its power to stick effectively to the existing surface as soon as it starts to set.

Figure 10.2

The plaster coats must be laid with uniform thickness, to give them sufficient structural strength to resist weathering and other erosive action. There are a number of special plastering tools, which are described briefly in the following paragraphs. A plastering specialist should have all these tools, since they all have a distinct purpose and assist in producing a really durable and attractive finish. However, for less important work it is possible to manage with a selection of them, since imported tools are often quite expensive. If the tools are available, they should be properly cleaned and washed after every use to ensure that they last and continue to give good service.

The mixed plaster is carried from the mortar board on a carrier known as a 'hawk'. The hawk is a metal platform about 25 to 30cm square supported on a vertical control handle, as shown below. The plasterer can hold the hawk in one hand and take plaster from it with a trowel held in his other hand. This saves him reaching up and down for each trowelful of mixed plaster, so saving time and allowing him to spread the plaster more evenly.

166

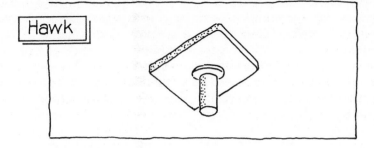

Figure 10.3

Plaster should be applied to the surface to be covered with a steel trowel, which is then used to spread and smooth the wet plaster. There are four main types of steel trowel, each with a separate purpose: these are illustrated below. The rectangular trowel, which has a blade about 10cm wide by 25cm long, is used for transferring the plaster on to the main surface and then for spreading the plaster. The pointing trowel, which is slightly smaller, can be used to get the plaster into corners where the rectangular trowel cannot be used. The margin trowel is also useful in awkward corners, with its square rather than pointed end. The angle trowel, with its sides turned up at right angles to the main blade, is valuable for finishing interior corner angles.

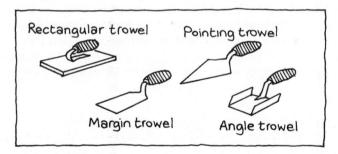

Figure 10.4

After the plaster has been spread and smoothed evenly over the surface, there is a finishing stage called 'floating', in which a tool called a float is run gently over the surface of the plaster to fill any small holes or hollows and leave it completely level, as well as leaving a suitable texture on the surface. Typical floats are illustrated in Figure 10.5. They are rather similar in size and appearance to a rectangular trowel, but with different surfaces to provide various textures. The wood float is probably the commonest, and is easiest to make, consisting of a flat rectangular piece of wood attached to a simple wooden handle. The sponge float is faced with foam rubber or plastic, and other variations can be faced with cork or carpet material to provide a range of finished textures. The angle float is made from sheet steel with its edges turned up, similarly to those of the angle trowel.

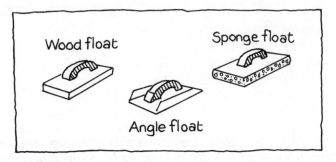

Figure 10.5

Other plastering tools in common use include the 'straight-edge' and the 'feather-edge' (Figure 10.6). The straight-edge consists of a handle attached to a metal or wooden blade 15cm wide and between $1\frac{1}{2}$ to 3 metres long, and is used to level and straighten the plaster. The feather-edge is similar, except that the blade tapers to a sharp edge so that it can be used to cut into corners and shape sharp straight lines.

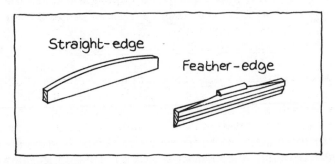

Figure 10.6

Another useful plastering tool is the 'darby', illustrated in Figure 10.7. It is effectively an extra long – about 1 metre – float, with two handles so that the user can apply pressure effectively.

It is used to finish levelling after the straight-edge has been used, and is used nearly flat against the plaster surface in such a way that the line of the edge makes an angle of about 45 degrees with the line of direction of the strokes.

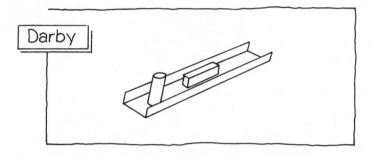

Figure 10.7

The only other tools needed are brushes to moisten the surface of the plaster, when it is being levelled, if necessary. A brush about 10cm wide and 5cm thick with bristles about 15cm long is usually convenient; a rather rough brush can be used for the base coat and a smoother one for the finishing coat.

Plaster is normally applied in two coats, each about ½cm thick, although three separate coats are sometimes used. It is a general rule that two thin coats of plaster perform better than one thick coat. In addition the surface of the wall to which the plaster coating is to be applied must be brushed clean of dust and loose matter, so that the plaster coating adheres firmly. Although careful preparation and application takes time, the occupier should remember that the materials are expensive, and good careful workmanship will mean that the surface coating will last for many years without having to be repaired or replaced.

Experimentation with the plaster mix is sometimes necessary, to ensure that the strength of the plaster coating matches that of the wall itself. Although it may seem that the stronger the coating, the better it will withstand the elements, in fact a coating which is stronger than the wall it covers is quite likely to crack seriously as it will expand and contract at a different rate with changes in temperature. Where the building is of more than one storey, some form of scaffolding will be necessary. To attempt to do without this is false economy, since plastering is a skilled operation and it cannot be done properly if the plasterer is attempting to balance on a heap of oil drums or some other ramshackle support.

169

Figure 10.8

The plaster must be mixed in small batches, so that it can be used soon after mixing. An hour is the maximum time that should be allowed to pass between first mixing the plaster and applying it to the wall. Whenever possible, the work should be carried out in one operation as joints can lead to weakness. Where there is no alternative to including joints because there is so much work to be done, they should be made carefully so that they look neat and do not allow water to penetrate and start a crack in the surface.

Vertical joints should never be made at corners. The plaster should be carried about 20cm around the corner, and a thin length of wood can be used to ensure a neat vertical joint with a uniform thickness of plaster.

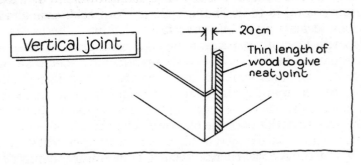

Figure 10.9

Horizontal joints must also be made with care. A common mistake is to taper down the surface of the upper layer of plaster. This may seem to be a way of leaving a neat temporary finish, but it results in the next layer tapering upwards and is therefore very vulnerable to water penetration and eventual cracking so that the plaster gradually peels away.

170

Figure 10.9 shows a better type of joint with a slight bevel outwards, so that water will be shed away from the joint and it will be protected. A useful way to ensure that this joint is properly formed is to plane off a bevel on the top edge of a strip of wood and nail it to the wall where the joint is required. Once again, a further benefit is that plastering up to the strip of wood ensures that there will be an even thickness of plaster at the joint.

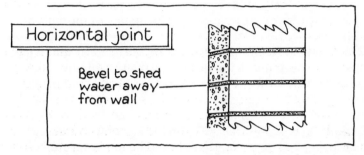

Figure 10.10

The plaster coating should be even and will look more attractive if it is smooth and flat. High spots can be evened out after the plaster has been applied, by moving the straight-edge over the surface to check their position and then using the 'darby' to flatten them. The float and steel trowel are then used to form a good surface. The trowel used for final finishing must be long and flat with a clean surface.

As with concrete, plaster will be much stronger if it is allowed to dry out slowly. So it is best to apply plaster to a shady side of a building, and spray or brush on water when it is starting to dry off so that it can cure gradually. If plaster has to be applied so that it faces the sun in the morning, it is a good idea to shade it in some way to avoid overrapid drying.

Normally, where concrete blocks or burnt brick walls are to be coated, only cement plaster is used. However, cement plaster can also be used on stable earth walls, although the surface must be properly prepared and walls containing a lot of clay are likely to swell and crack the coating. Surface coatings to earth walls must not be applied until the wall has dried out completely. With properly cured blocks, it is likely to take only a few weeks until the mortar dries; rammed earth, wattle and daub normally take much longer. This means that the walls must remain unprotected for quite a long time so, if the rainy season is

171

approaching, it is wise to include some form of stabilizer in the wall to give it extra protection.

Mud plaster
Mud plaster is much cheaper than cement plaster and can be quite effective as a plaster on earth walls, providing the material is suitable and it is properly applied. The most suitable material contains a proportion of approximately two parts sand to one part clay, and the red and brown laterite clays which are quite common in many African countries are particularly suitable.

It is possible to improve the performance of mud plasters by adding some form of stabilizer, such as cement or lime in a ratio of about one part stabilizer to nine or ten parts of soil. Again, it is best to experiment with various mixes to find out which gives the best result with the type of soil in the particular locality.

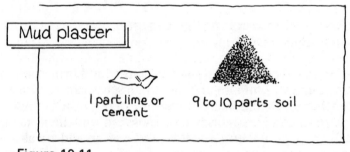

Figure 10.11

Paints and thin coatings
Paints and other thin coatings, such as cement slurries, can either be used on a plastered wall or applied directly as an alternative to a thicker and more expensive surface coating.

Slurries
A slurry is a mixture of cement and/or lime and water, brushed on to the wall with a large brush. Their useful life depends on the quality of the materials and workmanship, as well as the likely wear due to erosion and other damage. However, a properly applied slurry surface can last for five to ten years before it needs to be renewed.

As with other forms of coating, it is best to experiment with various types of mixture to see which is best, but equal amounts of lime and cement thoroughly mixed with enough water to form a thick liquid paste will probably be the best. If a gritty texture is

172

wanted, a small amount of clean, fine sand can be added. The slurry mixture must be thoroughly mixed before it is applied, and it is often necessary to stir it regularly with a stick while application is proceeding to ensure that none of the materials settle out and separate.

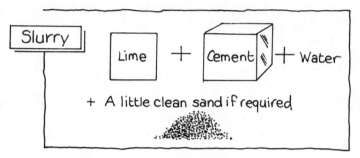

Figure 10.12

The wall must be suitable to take a slurry covering; earth walls, which are likely to shrink and swell significantly, are generally not suitable since they will be likely to first crack and then gradually peel off. The wall must be thoroughly cleaned before the slurry is applied, and it is advisable to moisten the wall first so that the slurry will be more likely to stick firmly when it is painted on. Usually, two coats of slurry will be needed to give adequate protection and a full day should be allowed to pass before the second coat is applied.

Paints

Painting has three main purposes. Firstly, it increases the life of the underlying surface by protecting it against moisture. Secondly, it makes the building look more attractive and therefore it becomes a more desirable place to live or work in. The third reason for painting is to improve sanitary conditions: a smooth, washable, painted surface can be cleaned far more easily than an unpainted one. A subsidiary purpose of painting is to improve lighting in a room by reflecting either natural or artificial light, or to increase the reflection of the sun's rays from outside surfaces to keep the building cooler than it would be otherwise.

All building materials are subject to attack by weather, as well as misuse by the occupiers and others on the premises. Their vulnerability, of course, varies considerably. Although steel is a very strong material in itself, it is very sensitive to a damp

173

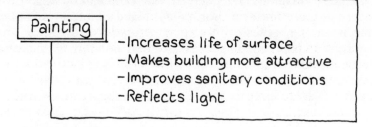

Painting
- Increases life of surface
- Makes building more attractive
- Improves sanitary conditions
- Reflects light

Figure 10.13

atmosphere and can rust rapidly if it is not properly protected. On the other hand, well-burnt bricks or the more resistant hardwoods will last for many years without any form of protection.

Paint is itself a building material. Although it cannot be described as a structural material, it is a necessary addition to structural building materials to ensure that the building in which they are incorporated performs as a satisfactory structure. It cannot be considered in isolation, but as a unit with whichever component it is used to coat.

A proper painting programme can have a significant impact on the life of a building and, since the preparation of the surface for painting and the application of the paint are both labour-intensive processes, this allows a real competitive advantage in the relative cost of protection to a developing country with lower wage rates. However, the cost of labour can only be ignored by the owner-occupier or the tenant who is required to repair and maintain his or her property as a condition of the lease, and it is important for any maintenance manager to look at the overall cost of the painting process as well as the cost per litre of paint.

Don't let the cost of paint hide the overall cost of the painting process

Figure 10.14

The cost and quantity of paint required to protect a building is quite small in relation to the costs and quantities of all other materials in the building. In fact, the approximate thickness of a single coat of paint is only about 0.01cm. Although the thickness of the layer is very thin, it can have a significant effect in increasing the useful life of the component which it covers. In fact, it is usual to increase the protection by applying more than one layer and, as with plastering, two or three thin layers are much more effective than one thick one.

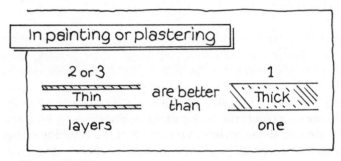

Figure 10.15

One of the difficulties in giving general advice on the optimum regularity and method of painting is due to the lack of observation and data on the results of painting in many countries. The first task of an individual who has been made responsible for maintenance is to gather evidence so that s/he can make judgements objectively. This data will probably have to be organized according to the type of building, and should lead to a proper examination of the costs of painting broken down into, for example, the following subheads:

Site preparation (scaffolding, ladders etc.)
Surface preparation
Painting materials
Cost of labour – applying paint.

This data should in turn lead to a rational assessment for each group of buildings of the most economical time to elapse before repainting; the most satisfactory type of paint to use and the best thickness and number of coats.

The most important principle in painting is to ensure that there is a good bond between the coat of paint and the surface to which it has been applied. If this bond is strong and highly resistant, the paintwork should continue to perform its protec-

175

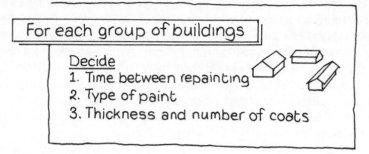

Figure 10.16

tive function for a considerable time before further treatment is required. However, once paint begins to flake or peel, immediate treatment is necessary. In fact, under these conditions it may be necessary to strip off the existing paintwork entirely, thereby adding to the additional cost. Thus, by careful preparation and the use of the right paint, the maintenance manager is wise to take care that adhesion at the interface of the component and its paint coating is as strong as possible.

Ideally, concern for painting should begin at the design stage, and the wise architect or engineer will call upon the maintenance supervisor for advice while the project is still on the drawing board. The chief enemy of a long-life paintcoat is water, and careful design can eliminate areas where rainwater can be trapped or condensation can occur. Paint films often swell when conditions are damp, causing a serious loss of adhesion which may be only partially recovered when the building dries out.

A further design factor which affects repainting costs is accessibility. Badly designed steel structures can cause severe problems, since they must be repainted regularly to ensure that

Figure 10.17

they retain adequate structural strength. Since it is often necessary to use a wire brush or scraper to prepare the surfaces, joints at acute angles which are difficult to reach should be avoided as a general rule.

Types of paint

Moving on from painting principles to painting practice two questions must be answered on each painting job:

What is the right paint?
How should it be applied?

The choice of the right paint for the job in hand is an important one, and is sometimes difficult with the wide range of types of paint that are now manufactured for specialist use. Most surfaces require three separate layers of paint to protect them properly: a primer to prepare the surface for painting, undercoat to provide a base for the finishing coat and a finishing coat for protection (and decoration).

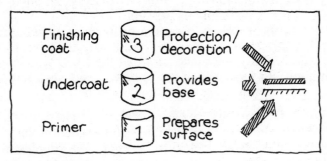

Figure 10.18

Primer. The purpose of the primer is to provide a surface on to which subsequent coats of paint will bond strongly. This reduces the risk of paint flaking away when it is dry and the need for repainting. On porous surfaces such as plaster or wood, the primer coat seals the surface and leaves it flat and smooth so as to prevent excessive absorption of further layers of paint. On metals, the primer has the job of rust-protection which prevents the metal from deterioration, discolouration and flaking. If a primer is not used, the later coats may not stick. Equally, if the wrong sort of primer is used, there will still be trouble ahead.

Different types of primer are available for different purposes. It is vital that the correct type is chosen to suit the job in hand. The idea that any old tin of paint found in the cupboard will do

177

for priming is quite wrong. The following list describes the primers recommended for various construction materials:

1. Softwoods. (including chipboard, blockboard and plywood). Any kind of wood primer will be satisfactory.
2. Hardwoods. Use an aluminium wood primer. In resinous woods, such as pine, any knots should first be treated with knotting (a special sealer to hold back the resin) otherwise the resin will gradually ooze out and damage the finished paintwork.
3. Plaster, concrete or brick surfaces. Use an alkali-resistant primer, sometimes described as a prime-sealer, acrylic primer or multi-purpose primer. If the surface is powdery or flaky, use a stabilizing or penetrating primer, sometimes described as a masonry sealer.
4. Iron and steelwork (including pipes and gutters). Use a calcium plumbate or red-lead primer. *Remember* that these are lead-based and poisonous, and so are potentially dangerous for interior work unless used in small quantities in rooms with good ventilation. For interior work a zinc chromate primer is preferable, sometimes called universal primer.

Care should be taken in choosing primers labelled 'universal primer', 'all-purpose primer' or 'multi-purpose primer'. Read the labels carefully and make sure that they are suitable for the job in hand. Surfaces which are to be emulsion-painted can be primed with a thinned-down emulsion paint.

Undercoat. Undercoats are easier to choose than primers, since the choice is related to the finishing coat that goes on top of them rather than the surface below the primer. The simplest way of choosing an undercoat is to have the same brand of product as the finishing coat and follow the manufacturer's recommendation.

A general rule is to use undercoat as close as possible in colour to the finish that is to go over it. More broadly still, white undercoat will be satisfactory for most pale colours while grey will suit most darker tones. What should be avoided is the use of a dark undercoat and a light finishing coat.

Finishing coat. Gloss paint gives a very durable finish which should not crack or chip, is easy to brush on and is suitable for use both inside and outside. The paint can be thinned, if necessary, with white spirit. To get a satisfactory finish, gloss paint must be thoroughly stirred before use.

If a tin is only partly-used, a skin is likely to form on the surface of the paint during storage. If this happens, cut round the skin with the point of a knife and lift it off, in one piece if possible. If the skin breaks up, it will be necessary to strain the paint before it is used. A good way to avoid 'skinning' is to store the tin of paint upside down – providing the lid is on firmly! In any case, the lid should always be pressed down firmly and the tin made airtight to protect the paint.

For a really hard-wearing finish, it is best to add a second coat of gloss paint, but only after allowing at least 24 hours for the first coat to harden.

Emulsion paint. Emulsion paint can provide a tough, smooth, washable, non-glossy surface whether used inside or outside. It is versatile and can be used over brickwork, plaster, wallboards and previously painted surfaces. A further advantage is that it dries quickly and can be recoated in one to four hours, depending on conditions.

It may be thinned with water to provide a sealing coat or to make it easier to apply to surfaces of high suction. Before thinning, the paint should be stirred to a smooth consistency. Then the water (up to one part of water to two parts of emulsion paint) should be added slowly whilst the mixture is stirred.

Brushes and tools

Buying a brush of the right size for the job is very important. Even a skilled painter will produce poor work if the brush is too wide or too narrow for the job in hand. The rules for buying a paintbrush are:

Get a brush of the right width.
Buy a good quality brush.
Keep it clean.
Use it properly.

The width for the job. A complete set of paintbrushes to suit most requirements would consist of:

1. A six-inch emulsion brush for walls and ceilings.
2. A three-inch brush for large areas such as the surfaces of flush doors.
3. A two-inch brush for moderate areas such as window sills, door frames, panelling and skirting. Possibly a one and a half inch brush would also be useful for woodwork less than three inches wide.
4. A one-inch brush is best for narrow areas such as window frames and door edges.
5. A narrow tapered sash brush with the bristles cut at an angle makes painting to a good line easier on glazing bars and wood-to-glass edges.

179

6. A pipe brush is useful for awkward work such as painting around water pipes and plumbing.

It is possible to speed up the job of painting by using a roller, particularly for large areas. However, rollers are sometimes more difficult to clean after use and can waste valuable paint, so most professional painters prefer to use brushes.

Buying a brush. It is wise to pay a little extra and invest in good quality brushes which will give better results and last longer. A clean, soft brush of good quality can last for years, and is cheaper in the long run than a series of 'cheap' brushes that wear out quickly and have to be replaced.

Keeping it clean. There is no point in buying good quality brushes unless they are cared for properly after use; this takes only a little time and effort. The alternatives are bringing a hard, uncleaned, paint-impregnated brush back to life which takes much time, or else buying a replacement.

The brush should be cleaned immediately after use. The first step is to squeeze out the excess paint by laying the brush on a piece of old newspaper and scraping down the bristles with a thin piece of wood or an old knife. Any remaining loose paint can then be brushed out, and the brush cleaned with turpentine, white spirit or a proprietary cleaner. The fingers can be used to ensure that the cleaner is well worked into the bristles, and it is most important to make sure that all the paint has been removed from the base of the bristles. Finally, the brush should be washed out in warm water with soap or a detergent, and rinsed until the water runs clean. When the brush has dried out, it can be stored flat in a dry cool place until it is needed again.

For short-term storage between painting sessions the brush can be hung in linseed oil, turpentine or paint solvent; it should not be left standing on its bristles. A good way to avoid this is to drill a hole in the handle and hang the brush on a piece of string short enough to ensure that the bristles are clear of the bottom of the container. Before re-use the excess solvent should be wiped out with a rag or removed by brushing.

Using the paint brush. Good painting consists of three operations – getting the paint on to the surface, working it into the surface and removing the excess paint. The great advantage of using a brush is that after it has spread the paint on the surface the natural action of the bristles works the paint into the surface below. This applies to primer, undercoat and gloss paint. After the paint has been placed on the surface, the skilled painter will

180

go over it with long, light strokes in one direction to obliterate the brush marks and leave a smooth, clean finished surface. Long sweeping strokes are most effective in leaving an even surface. The freshly-dipped brush should first be placed in an area which already contains wet paint, since the fresh paint softens that which is already on the wall and prevents marks between strokes.

Few people really enjoy painting, and many are tempted to complete the job quickly by putting too much paint on the brush and applying a thick coat of paint, so as to avoid the need for additional coats. These habits lead to a finish of poor quality and durability.

Overloading the brush with paint slows the job down in the long run, as drips have to be cleaned up and paint runs off the bristles on to the handle. Ideas such as putting rag round the handle to catch the drips do not work very well, the real answer is simply to pick up a moderate amount of paint each time the brush is dipped into the paint. A good tip is to tie a piece of wire across the centre of the top of the tin, and after each dip wipe one edge of the brush across the wire to remove the excess paint. It is a mistake to wipe off excess paint against the side of the tin as the channel at the top of the tin fills up, leading to spillage and difficulty in replacing the lid properly. If moderate amounts of paint are used, it should be possible to avoid drips even when working with the brush upside down on surfaces like the top of a window frame.

As pointed out earlier in the chapter, two or three thin layers of paint give better – and therefore longer – protection than one thick one. Thick layers dry unevenly, assuming that they dry at all. The top surface will not harden properly and will tend to produce a rippled effect. If it does eventually harden it will dry unevenly, and will tend to crack and flake away. An indication that too much paint is being put on in a single layer is a tendency for the paint to 'run' on vertical surfaces or to form puddles on horizontal surfaces.

Preparing for painting

There are no short cuts to preparing a surface for painting, but time spent in careful preparation pays off in the long run by ensuring a long-lasting finish. As a guide, it is likely to take just as long to prepare the surface as to paint it, or, looking at it another way, when the brush is dipped into the paint-can for the first time, the job of painting should be half-finished!

Before applying fresh coats of paint the underlying surface

181

must be stable and clean. Any trace of grease or wax polish must be cleaned off thoroughly, otherwise the paint will be slow to dry and possibly prone to peeling and flaking. Rust must be removed from metal surfaces by chipping, scraping and using a wire-brush. As soon as the surface is clean and bright a special metal primer (as discussed earlier) should be applied immediately so that no further rust formation can occur.

If most of the existing paint on woodwork is badly crazed or blistered, or has started to flake away, it will be necessary to burn off the existing paint completely to give a good surface. But if there are only small areas of defective paint, they can be removed by using a metal scraper and rubbing down the surface firmly with sandpaper. If there are cracks or old nail holes in the surface, these should be cut out and made good with a filler. After the filler has dried, the surface should be sanded down and primed.

All traces of dust and dirt should be washed off the surface before starting to paint. It may be necessary to use paint thinner and then wash with soap and water or a detergent solution to remove heavy films of grease or wax polish. Where ordinary dust and dirt are the problem, soap and water or detergent solution alone should be enough to get the surface clean. Remember to always *rinse* the surface with clean water after washing and allow plenty of time for the surface to *dry* before painting. Dampness itself is a major cause of flaking and blistering.

When painting windows take particular care to clean the dirt from around the edges of the frames and to wipe off the dirt which tends to gather around the glazing bars. If this dirt is difficult to remove with soap and water, it may be necessary to clean it off with a rag soaked in turpentine.

Eight preparations

1. *Don't* paint over a flaking or blistered surface – the paint just will not stick!
2. *Don't* paint over dirt or grease – the paint will take too long to dry and the work will look shoddy!
3. *Don't* paint on a wet surface – the paint will flake or blister!
4. *Don't* paint over an old coat of thick, soft paint – the new coat will blister!
5. *Don't* sweep the floors just before (or during) painting – the dust will ruin your new paint!
6. *Don't* use a dirty paintbrush – it will spoil your new paintwork!

7. *Don't* forget to remove the skin from paint that has been used before – it will break up and leave bits of old skin on the new surface!

8 *Don't* forget to read the instructions on the paint tin – they were put there for a purpose!

Figure 10.19

Before starting to paint the outside of a building, check first that the structure is sound and no repairs or maintenance are needed. Remember to examine and clean out the guttering. If the gutters are made of metal, the inside should be coated with bituminous paint. One great advantage of plastic guttering and downpipes is that they do not need painting.

Using a ladder

Painting is a skilled job. It cannot be done properly if the painter balances precariously on an old oil drum or a pile of bricks. To work properly you need scaffolding or a ladder. Even working from a ladder can be dangerous if it is not used properly, and better work will result if a little extra time is spent in making sure that the ladder is in the right place and will not slip.

The ladder should be at the right slope, secure at the top and secure at the toe. The best slope for a ladder is 1:4. That means that the toe of the ladder should be 1 metre from the wall if it is 4 metres high.

A good tip with regard to buildings that will have to be maintained regularly is to put screw eyes into the fascia board, so that the top rung of the ladder can be tied to them and held firmly. The screw eyes are quite cheap to buy and can be painted over so that they will be ready for use next time. Never rest the top of the ladder against the guttering – it could break or buckle, causing the ladder to fall.

The toe of the ladder should be firmly wedged so that there is no danger of it sliding away. On soft ground a peg can be hammered into the ground and tied to the bottom rung to stop it sinking when the painter starts to climb.

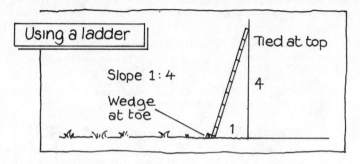

Figure 10.20

It is useful to have a ladder hook or platform attached to the ladder to carry the paint can. No one can produce good work with a paint can in one hand and a brush in the other while trying to keep balanced at the same time. Unless the painter is left-handed, s/he should always start at the right-hand side of the work and move the ladder steadily to the left in stages, so that there is never any need to prop the ladder against a newly-painted surface.

Planning the painting job
Painting work can be made quicker and more efficient by careful planning. The first step is to go round the building carefully, check that all other repair and maintenance work is complete and decide on the surfaces to be painted. Next comes the decision on the number of coats of paint to be applied, the type of paint to be used and the colour scheme. It is best to avoid too many different colours and types of paints on a single job because this will mean that more paint will be left over at the end of the work and more time will be spent cleaning brushes when the painter has to switch to a different paint.

The next step is to work out how much paint of various kinds will be needed to complete the job. Most paint tin labels give an indication of the area which should be covered per litre of paint, but it is wise to add a small percentage (say ten per cent) to the calculated quantity to avoid having the job held up near the end while an extra tin of paint is bought from the merchant.

It is not necessary to carry out a precise mathematical calculation of the area of wood on every window and door

184

frame. A rough estimate is enough and an experienced painter will be able to estimate paint requirements with surprising accuracy. Suppose that the areas for a painting job are calculated as follows:

			sq.m
Gloss	Doors and frames (both sides)	15 @ 5 sq.m =	75
Coat	Windows	20 @ 2 sq.m =	40
	Skirting board	=	15
	Other surfaces	=	40
			170
	ADD 10 per cent allowance		17
			187

Assume that coverage is:
Undercoat: 1 litre should cover 11 sq. m.
Gloss finish: 1 litre should cover 17 sq. m.
Litres of undercoat required

$$= \frac{187}{11} \qquad = 17 \text{ litres}$$

Litres of gloss required

$$= \frac{187}{17} \qquad = 11 \text{ litres}$$

'Guesstimate' of primer required

$$= 2 \text{ litres}$$

Emulsion	Area of walls and ceiling	= 200
	ADD 10 per cent allowance	20
		220

Assume coverage: 1 litre should cover 15 sq. m.
Allow for two coats.
Therefore, litres of emulsion required

$$= \frac{2 \times 220}{15}$$

$$= 30 \text{ litres approximately}$$

Before buying the paint, the brushes and tools should be checked over to make sure that they are all fit to be used and that no additional purchases need to be made. Also decide whether any additional paint thinners or cleaners are required.

The next stage is preparation. Remember to do this thoroughly so that the paint will have a chance to provide maximum protection. Any cracked or loose putty around window frames should be replaced, and cracks and nail holes filled and smoothed down. The general principle when cleaning is to work from the top downwards so that dirt and debris from the area being cleaned can never spoil the areas that have already been dealt with.

Finally, decide on the order of work before beginning. Again, the principle is that it is always best to start at the top and work downwards. On inside work this means that the ceiling should always be the first priority. When painting the ceiling it is best to work methodically in narrow strips so that successive strips are painted alongside areas that have not yet dried thus avoiding lap marks.

After the ceiling, the next job is the walls. These are usually the easiest surfaces to paint since areas are large and uninterrupted and the painter can usually stand on the floor to do the work. The best place to begin is at an upper corner of the wall. Then work along the edge of the ceiling for about one metre. Next work down the corner steadily, always keeping the painted strip in line. After that the walls can be completed using broad sweeping strokes and working from wet to dry areas so as to avoid lap marks.

After the walls are complete, the woodwork can be painted. When painting doors, start with the frames, then do the edges before starting on the main door surface. The general rule of 'top to toe' still applies – when painting each part start at the top and work downwards to avoid dripping paint on to the finished work. When painting complicated woodwork, like a panelled door, it is worthwhile to decide on the order of painting in advance.

In general, it is best to paint the vertical surfaces before the horizontal surfaces, but look carefully at how the woodwork was assembled by the carpenter in the first place. If one piece of woodwork butts against another piece, like a side road meeting a main road at a 'T' junction, then the 'side road' should be painted before the 'main road'. This allows the painter to get a clean, straight finish across the joint.

When painting of primer or undercoat is complete, leave enough time for it to dry before applying the next coat. Drying times are usually stated on the paint tin, but 24 hours is usually enough (or about four or five hours if emulsion paint is being used). If children of people who do not know that painting is in progress are likely to pass near the area being painted, remember to put up a warning sign or barrier so that they will not accidentally touch the paint while it is still wet.

CHAPTER 11
Building Services

Building services can be defined as those systems and their components which provide plumbing, sewerage, heating, ventilation, air conditioning, lighting, power, vertical transport, fire protection, and special services such as public address or oxygen to a building.[1] The design of these systems and their components requires many skills and close co-operation between the design team, client and maintenance team to ensure that the installations are economic, durable and maintainable. All services should be readily accessible and adequate working space should be provided to enable maintenace and repair work to be carried out conveniently and economically.

Economy
Designers of building services should (like other designers) consider the relative importance of initial and running costs, as well as the life-cycle cost of alternative designs. It is worth noting that a high maintenance cost may well be appropriate for components which are subject to obsolescence, for instance where a component needs to be changed every few years. So an economic balance has to be struck to determine the increase in initial costs that may be justified by a reduction in maintenance costs. Various methods of evaluating design alternatives have already been discussed in chapter 2.

Durability
Durability refers to the life-expectancy of the facility or component. Some services may be expected to last the whole life of the building and, indeed, any failure of such services is likely to be serious both functionally and economically. Other services will not last the whole life of the building, and the periodic renewal of minor items such as light bulbs, ball valves and so on is inevitable. Experience or testing generally provides the design team with all the information that is required. Often, however, there may be variability in quality of workmanship, or

1. Robert J. Reichert, 'Guide to Real Estate Terminology', *Real Estate and Research*, (Palmerston North, New Zealand, 1982).

187

the conditions of exposure or use may be uncertain, and short-term or accelerated tests may give misleading indications. Only tentative judgement may be be possible, based on technical knowledge and subject to confirmation in due course, by observation. This underscores the need to keep proper maintenance records and to have information feedback.

Maintainability
In many buildings the majority of the services are concealed in ducts, trenches, false ceilings and elsewhere, and access may become a problem unless full information is provided by the design team. This should be effectively cross-referenced so that maintenance staff or service engineers do not have to take down a whole ceiling in search of a single control device, valve or drain-point.

Pipes and fittings should be accessible after installation for purposes of inspection, servicing, repairs or replacement. Pipes below solid floors should preferably be laid in channels covered with access panels, or else encased behind skirtings set forward from the wall's face. Vertical pipes may be fixed in recesses in walls faced with removable panels. Exposed pipework provides maximum accessibility but is often resisted on aesthetic grounds, although it may not be too objectionable if fixed to follow skirtings, architraves and similar features.[2] Concealment in cupboards provides accessibility and eliminates the problem of appearance.

Four useful design tips to assist in achieving maintainability (and safety for operatives and the maintenance team) are:

1. Sufficient space should be left between the pipework and its housing to allow the pipe to be painted after installation.
2. The layout of service pipe and cable runs should be planned so that joints in liquid-carrying pipe-runs are not placed over electrical equipment.
3. Areas where there is machinery or electric current should be well-lit and have adequate space for maintenance to be safely carried out.
4. Manhole covers to inspection chambers of surface water, soil drainage or underground tanks holding effluent should not be locked.

Specialized services
There are many different types of specialist service which may be installed in a single building and for which there will be need

2. Ivor H. Seeley, *Building Maintenance*, (Macmillan Press Ltd, 1976).

for maintenance. Such maintenance needs may be governed by statutory regulations or manufacturers' specifications. Regulations (or at least their interpretation) vary from area to area, and are also liable to change. Thus, it is necessary for the maintenance staff or service engineers to keep up to date on current regulations and to check outlines and detailed intentions.

These specialist installations are often maintained through maintenance contracts with installers, suppliers or specialist companies, and include the following:

1. Communications systems, including telephones; alarm systems; intercom devices and public address systems for conference facilities.
2. Vertical transport systems, including all systems for lifting people and goods such as lifts, escalators, hoists and cranes.
3. Air-conditioning equipment. In addition to heating and ventilating equipment, an air-conditioning system will have refrigeration plant and, in some cases, equipment for humidity control. The testing and balancing of this equipment is best left to installers, suppliers or specialist companies.
4. Fire-fighting equipment. Building regulations specify the provision of adequate escape routes, fire alarms, extinguishers and adequate lighting of escape routes. In addition to these requirements, automatic fire detection and extinguishing equipment may be installed in important public buildings. Whatever the type of equipment, regular testing and maintenance is essential. This is usually done through maintenance contracts with local fire services or specialist contractors.

Maintenance contracts

Whatever type of equipment is installed, it will need to be maintained throughout its life so as to satisfy user needs and retain the same standard of performance at minimum cost. It is prudent to consult a reputable manufacturer from the start and equally important to obtain the services of a reputable company to maintain the equipment. Many manufacturers and specialist companies offer a range of maintenance packages depending on the needs of the equipment. Essentially two forms of maintenance contract may be offered. The choice between them will depend partly on cost, but many organizations prefer comprehensive contracts for key equipment as this minimizes the risk of additional costs, delays and possible danger while it is out of action.

1. A comprehensive maintenance contract. This is an all-embracing service including regular inspection and service according to statutory requirements or manufacturers' specifi-

189

cations, based on principles of preventive maintenance. The aim is to prolong the life of the equipment and maintain optimum performance. Any repair work or replacement will be carried out as necessary, and emergency works would be attended to promptly as soon as the company is notified. The period of the contract may be annual or up to five years.

2. A basic maintenance contract. The contracting firm carries out regular inspection, servicing and minor repairs which can be done on the premises without requiring new parts or use of special equipment. Emergency work can be carried out only during normal working hours, and any calls outside these hours must be paid for as extra charge. The company, however, will report to the customer if any work is required which falls outside the scope of the agreement.

Plumbing and electrical services
The most common building services are plumbing and electrical installations. Both can give rise to serious trouble if they are not inspected regularly, and promptly and competently maintained. Leakage from plumbing installations is both wasteful and potentially damaging to the building fabric, while faulty electrical circuits can be a source of mortal danger to the occupants. The remainder of this chapter will focus on common defects affecting plumbing and electrical services.

Plumbing
This heading includes domestic water installations, soil and waste installations and sanitary appliances, including taps and valves.

Water services. From the treatment plant, water is fed to the supply areas where a ring main network of pipes is located. These pipes have stop-valves at every 100 metres and at branch junctions. From the mains supply, water is led to individual dwellings in 12mm diameter pipes (or larger pipes depending on the building's size and the number of occupants). From the boundary stop-valve the supply pipe is extended to the building. To prevent damage by traffic and weather, the supply-pipe is placed 750mm below the ground until it is inside the building. A stop-valve is placed immediately above ground-floor level, and from this the supply pipe rises to a cistern in the roof. Pipes that take water from the cistern are called distribution pipes; they take water to outlets such as sinks, toilets, baths, showers and hot-water storage cylinders.

The water enters the cistern through a ball-valve, and all distribution pipes are provided with stop-valves at the bottom of the cistern. The cistern also has an overflow pipe to discharge water outside the building in the event of an overflow.

Maintenance of water services. The maintenance of mains services by water authorities ends at the boundary stop-valve. So building owners and occupiers are always responsible for the maintenance of the supply-pipes and appliances within building boundaries. Experience shows that the most common maintenance problems in water services can be traced to defective ball-valves and leaking taps.

Ball-valves and taps. Some of the most common failures affecting ball-valves are perforated floats, eroded seating, defective washers or the presence of grit. Soldered copper floats may become corroded so that the float breaks away or becomes perforated, this is one reason for the inreasing use of plastic floats. The high-velocity discharge of water from a ball-valve may erode the seating and cause leaks. The remedial measure would be to install a new seating or reseat the valve with a special stool. Defective washers should be replaced as soon as leakage is evident. The remedial action against grit deposits is simply to dismantle the ball-valve and clean it.

Pipes. Besides valves and taps, the supply and distribution pipes may leak, too, mainly at the joints. The joint may not have been properly made, or could corrode due to the jointing of dissimilar metals, or to chemical action and thermal movements. Remedial actions include remaking the joints, renewing corroded parts, and redesigning the piping system with bends and loops to shorten the lengths of straight pipe which can shorten or lengthen appreciably due to variations in temperature.

Cisterns. These are usually made from galvanized steel, copper or plastic, although fibre concrete (FC) tanks are a recent alternative. Many failures of galvanized steel tanks occur due to bimetallic action where the cistern has been joined to copper pipes. Acid or soft water may attack zinc so that it no longer protects the steel from corrosion. If the tank rusts and leaks badly, there is no alternative to replacement, but a single leak may be patched and the whole interior of the tank painted with bitumen paint. The alternative is to use plastic or fibre concrete tanks which cannot rust.

Hot-water supply systems. Hot-water cylinders and pipes are usually made of galvanized steel or copper. Apart from defects

191

common to cisterns and cold-water pipes, there are a number of defects that frequently occur in hot-water systems:

1. Air-locks arising from trapped air in the system that impedes the flow of water from the cylinder to the appliances. To remove the air, blow through the pipework or release the air by draining and refilling the tank.
2. Insufficient hot water, arising from an inadequate size of boiler or hot-water cylinder, excessive lengths of distribution pipes, insufficient insulation of pipes and cylinders or air-locks.
3. Noises arising from the expansion of water by freezing, furring or corrosion. Excessive water hardness may lead to the gradual furring-up of pipes and loss of performance in heat exchangers. The extent of furring should therefore be checked regularly.

Fittings. These include baths, lavatory basins, sinks and water closets. Water closets and lavatory basins are made of ceramic materials (glazed earthenware, glazed fireclay and vitreous china). Defects in water closets include persistent slow filling due to blockage; inadequate flushing due to the cistern not being properly filled, or a perforated float. The remedies are to clear blockages, replace ball-valves and corroded cisterns. If inadequate flushing is caused by an obstruction in the flush pipe, this may need to be checked. Baths and sinks are made from ceramic materials, cast iron, fibre-glass or plastic. Problems sometimes arise with drainage and overflows which are usually difficult to clean, resulting in an unpleasant stench when the waste plug is lifted.

Drainage services. These refer to soil drains and surface-water drains. Soil drains take sewage and other effluents from the building to the main sewer, septic tank or cesspool. Surface-water drains carry rainwater to main sewers, soakaways or stormwater drains. These drainage systems are usually governed by public health regulations, which vary from country to country.

Defects in drainage services. Leakage of water or effluent from drainage systems can either be through cracks in damaged pipes or at the joints. The incorrect bedding of pipes may cause failure of the joints and even cracking of the pipes. Concrete and asbestos pipes may be attacked by sulphates in clay soils and made-up ground, resulting in pipes becoming porous or breaking-up completely. Particular care should be taken in bedding and laying pipes and ensuring that trenches are carefully back-filled.

The accumulation of silt, grease and solid matter can lead to serious problems, including flooding. Inspection pits, interceptors and other access points in the drainage system should be inspected and cleaned regularly. Where it is necessary to pump up effluent to the level of the main sewer, daily checking is necessary in addition to regular maintenance of the pumps. Where sewage is disposed of on-site by septic tanks and soakaways, it will be necessary to pump out and remove sludge at regular intervals. Manhole covers should also be inspected regularly for damage, as broken covers can be a source of danger.

Electrical installations

The supply of electricity is usually governed by power acts, and it is distributed by electricity or power boards which provide guidance on installation techniques and safety precautions. Power, from whatever source, is generally distributed by overhead cables carried on pylons at very high voltages. At points along the lines, the voltage is stepped down at transformer substations, then distributed through smaller substations to domestic, commercial and industrial premises. The incoming wires to a building comprise a live insulated phase conductor and an insulated neutral conductor which is earthed at the nearest substation. The cable enters the building close to the service position, that is, a board on to which is mounted a meter and cut-out equipment belonging to the electricity board. From the meter the power is led to the consumer's service unit; this is a metal box containing a main switch and fuse-board. The fuse-board has a number of fuses for each appliance in the building, including cooker and heater sockets, power points and lighting circuits.

The wiring in the building could be tough rubber-sheathed or PVC-sheathed cables, vulcanized rubber-insulated or PVC-insulated cables or mineral-insulated copper-sheathed cable.

It is important to designate all cable-runs before construction starts, and to make provision for their easy insertion. Cables that are buried in plaster or other materials should be within conduits, while those between floor joints or in the roof space need only be tough rubber-sheathed cables. The method of housing cables in concrete floors depends on the construction. Conduit, metal or plastic trunking or ducts from inflatable tubes may be adopted, and these should preferably be placed on top of the floor within a screed. Within *in-situ* solid slabs, the conduit can be placed on the formwork, and drops through such a floor to lighting points, and vertical ducts must be formed by shuttering. Conduit should always be laid to a slight fall, so that any condensation and water that accumulates during construction can be drained off before the cable is inserted.

Maintenance of electrical systems

Power systems up to the service position remain the property of the electricity board. From thereon the wiring becomes the responsibility of the consumer. Electrical wiring deteriorates due to the ageing of the insulation material and cumulative mechanical damage, and should be inspected and tested regularly, preferably every five years. It will be necessary to break walls, floors and so on for any repairs to be done where wiring is concealed in the building fabric. Detailed wiring and location diagrams should therefore be kept readily available for ease of identification and access.

Lamps and fittings not only have to be replaced, but should also be cleaned at regular intervals. The frequency of replacement will depend on the burning hours per year, but as a guide, tubes that work 100 hours per week may need to be replaced every twelve months, while those that work for a quarter of this time should only need to be replaced every four years.

CHAPTER 12

Earthquakes and Cyclones

Buildings are usually designed and constructed to cope with the stresses and strains that they will have to face from the everyday activities of the occupants, the normal range of climatic conditions and the weight of the materials used in construction. There are areas of the world which can experience climatic conditions of unusual and extreme ferocity, such as earthquakes and cyclones. As their arrival and impact are very difficult to predict, designers and building owners and occupiers are often tempted to ignore the potential threat that they represent.

It is true that total earthquake or cyclone resistance is both difficult and expensive to achieve. Yet there are measures which can be taken at a reasonable cost which will increase resistance to damage and give the occupants a reasonable chance of survival. It has been estimated that to erect an earthquake-resistant building instead of a normal one of good quality would add from two to seven per cent to its cost. This modest increase must be weighed against the potential damage and loss of life which an earthquake can cause in settlements where the buildings are inadequate.

Ideally it would be preferable if people did not have to settle in areas which are susceptible to earthquake or cyclone damage. The difficulty is that it is impossible to predict the areas at risk with any degree of precision, and there are a number of countries in which such damage could occur at any location within their national boundaries. Charles Richter, the inventor of the 'Richter scale' for measuring the intensity of earthquakes, periodically reminds his fellow Californians that there is 'no locality in California which is safe from earthquake risk'. In such areas there is no safe place to live from the aspect of minimizing risk. Thus the property owner, the occupier, the builder and the maintainer of buildings must allow for and live with the risks. Above all, they must remember that the risk is there. Just as it is difficult to know which horse will win a race, although it is certain that one of the horses will win, it is difficult to guess where an earthquake is most likely to occur – but it is certain that earthquakes will continue to occur *somewhere*.

Designers must recognize the risks, and take appropriate action. The first step is to define priorities, and the top priority should be to protect the occupiers as far as possible from the risk of injury or even loss of life. The second priority is to minimize the expected cost of repair to damage in relation to a realistic extra initial capital cost. Some damage, such as cracks and broken windows, is inevitable and must be accepted if there is a major earthquake.

A more difficult question is that of setting priorities between buildings. This is even harder to decide when earthquakes are the risk rather than cyclones. Some warning of cyclones is usually available, and vulnerable public buildings can be cleared. But earthquakes are more sudden and if a school collapses during school hours many children's lives will be lost. Other public buildings and structures, including power stations, water facilities and public halls for emergency accommodation may also have to be given priority in the general interest of the community. If public funds are not available to assist in strengthening private homes, it is still a government responsibility to make the risks clear so that everyone is properly aware of the danger involved.

There are intense extremes of heat and cold in many earthquake regions, and many houses are built with mud walls up to one metre thick for good insulation. Because of the shortage of wood, walls and roofs are virtually unsupported. Thus even the vibrations and shock from a small earthquake will bring the roof crashing down, crushing or asphyxiating the people in the rooms below. Even when reinforced concrete is employed in more modern buildings, designers may not use it to the best advantage. For example, failure to strengthen the corners and intersections with an appropriate amount of extra steel may prove fatal – the failure of a multi-storey concrete block will cause many more casualties than that of a series of simple single-storey structures.

A good design will not provide a safe structure if the builder is careless or unqualified. If the specification and local building codes are ignored by the contractor and supervision is sporadic and lax, as is often the case, design factors of safety will be diminished in practice and the building will collapse under stresses which would normally be withstood. The use of inadequate materials is particularly dangerous. Even the use of contaminated or salt-water in the mixing of concrete can seriously reduce the strength of the concrete and endanger the building and its occupants. When the reinforcing bar is of a

196

smaller cross-section than specified, or even omitted altogether, the effect is yet more serious. Money and time spent on close supervision is seldom wasted in the long run.

This book is not intended to provide an exhaustive treatise on earthquake resistance, although some of the general principles to be observed are set down in the following pages. An excellent practical treatment of this matter is to be found in *Small Buildings in Earthquake Areas*[1] from which much of the information in this chapter is drawn.

Design principles

Shape. Simple round, square or rectangular buildings perform best in earthquakes. Long, thin buildings or T- or L- shaped blocks have the worst record. If the client's requirements or the site configuration dictates that a T- or L- shape should be adopted, it is better to make it up from two *separate* rectangular-shaped buildings with a gap of at least 100 mm between them.

Openings. Openings in the building should be reasonably symmetrical: it is bad practice to have all the doors and windows at the front and a plain wall at the back, or vice-versa. A good basic design for a two-room dwelling would be as illustrated in Figure 12.1 with a squarish rectangular plan shape and the door and window openings spaced out along the two longer walls at the front and the back. In general, openings should be kept as small as possible and should not be close to each other or to corners or intersections of walls.

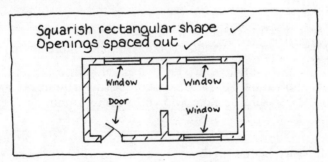

Figure 12.1

Tying the building together. Any building which may be shaken or subject to stress from external forces such as cyclones or earthquakes needs to be more firmly tied together than a

1. Daldy, A.F. *Small Buildings in Earthquake Areas* (Building Research Establishment, UK, 1972).

building which has only to withstand more normal stresses. If walls are not connected together firmly, they crack at the corners at the first shock, then separate and collapse at the second shock. If the roof is not tied-in to the walls, they will spread out at the top and the roof will collapse on the people underneath. The major extra cost involved in making a building earthquake-resistant is that of tying it together satisfactorily and reinforcing the places where different parts of the building are joined together.

Where to reinforce. The first priority is to stop the top of the walls spreading outwards to prevent the roof from collapsing. The best way to do this for blockwork, masonry or burnt-brick walls is to construct a reinforced conrete ring-beam around the top of the walls. In a two-storey building, a second ring-beam will be needed at first-floor level.

The next desirable step is to provide vertical reinforcement wherever two walls meet. This should join into the foundation and the ring-beam at roof level, so as to provide a complete framework, strengthening all the edges of the building.

If the earthquake risk is severe, the third priority is to provide vertical reinforcement at the sides of all doors and windows, and horizontal reinforcement in layers inside the walls. Wherever bars overlap or cross they should be *fixed together securely*.

Steel reinforcement is expensive so it should be placed where it will be most effective. If money is short, or the risk not severe, remember the order of priority:

Ring beam
Vertical reinforcement where walls meet
Sides of doors and windows or horizontal reinforcement in walls.

It is also worthwhile to include steel reinforcement in the footings of buildings in areas subject to earthquakes and it is vital they should be taken down to firm ground.

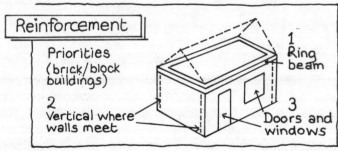

Figure 12.2

Uniformity. Once the building has been designed, good supervision is crucial to ensure that all materials are up to standard. In an earthquake, a building is as strong (or weak) as its weakest part. The weakest part may be a batch of poorly burnt bricks that were included in one section of the walls or it may be an area that was set in a batch of bad mortar. What matters is *not* the average quality, but the quality of the weakest component. There is no way that one batch of above-average quality material can compensate for a batch which is below average. The builder and the supervisor must aim for *uniformity*, with a uniform quality-level at or above that set in the specification.

Strengthening earth walls

Earth walls have great advantages, particularly in dry areas. They can be thickly built to give excellent protection against extremes of heat or cold, and they are cheap because they employ local materials and do not require specialist building skills. However, they are dangerous in earthquake areas if they are built without any form of reinforcement, as they are structurally weak and prone to collapse during tremors.

A simple way to reinforce earth walls is to incorporate buttresses at the time of construction. The addition of buttresses to a finished structure will not work as they will not bond effectively with the existing building, the result being that the buttresses are likely to shrink away from the wall as they dry out. The way buttresses *should* be set out is illustrated in Figure 12.3. Two buttresses should be constructed at each corner of the building (one in line with each wall). Additional intermediate buttresses will be needed wherever a cross wall meets an external wall, and opposite any arch which supports a heavy roof.

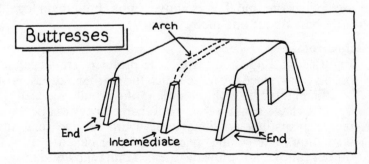

Figure 12.3

Wattle and daub walls are cheap and quite popular in hot, wet climates. A serious disadvantage is that the strength of these walls can deteriorate over the years due to rot or decay of the timber and attack by termites. Thus the structure, although initially sound, may have been weakened considerably by the time it is subject to an earthquake tremor. If the roof is heavy, such as a thatched roof, the danger will be intensified. If cost considerations dictate this form of construction, it is best to choose a lightweight roof and reinforce the walls with steel angle-irons, bars and rods.

An effective way to do this is to fix the angle irons vertically at the corners of the building and at other wall intersections. The angles should extend from the top of the wall to at least 0.75 m below ground level and should be at least of section 75 x 75 x 6 mm. The tops of the angles should be fixed together with flat steel bars at least 75 x 6 mm welded to them; and 12 mm diameter steel rods fixed diagonally across the rooms under the ceiling and welded to the angles.

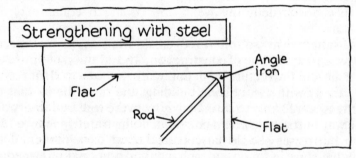

Figure 12.4

Where roofs consist of long semicircular arches, diagonal tie-bars would not be practicable. The best alternative in this case is to use angle irons and flats as above, but to hold them together with tie-bars about one metre apart.

Pitched roofs

1. Light roofs. Light roofs are to be preferred in earthquake-prone areas, since the force which the earthquake exerts on a building increases with the weight of the building itself. It is better to have a lightweight roof than a heavy one, even if it means providing a ceiling underneath to give reasonable insulation. The ceiling sheets should be nailed well to the timber above to prevent them falling down during an earthquake shock.

The roof must be firmly joined to the walls by bolting the wallplates to the ring-beam. The main additional point to remember in earthquake areas is to be sure that the wall plates, rafters, purlins and other roof timbers are all fixed together in accordance with normal good practice.

2. Tiled roofs. Tiled roofs are naturally much heavier than corrugated sheet-covered roofs, and consequently need much more timber-framing to support them. There are three rules of special importance in earthquake areas:

   (i)   The ties at ceiling level must be strong enough to prevent the roof from spreading.
   (ii) The wall plates must be firmly fixed to the ring-beam.
   (iii) The rafters and trusses must be fixed to the wallplate.

3. Thatched roofs. Thatched roofs are also heavy, particularly when wet since they absorb moisture readily. There is a need for ties to hold the roof together at the level of the top of the wall, particularly where the slope has been made steep so that the roof will be watertight. The provision of a ring-beam is also very helpful.

Flat roofs

1. Reinforced concrete roofs. Providing they are properly designed and constructed, with sufficient steel reinforcement tied into the remainder of the reinforced concrete framework, these roofs should form a satisfactory covering to the more modern forms of building. However, if a building with a reinforced concrete roof does collapse, it is likely to be catastrophic, so there is a crucial need for competent design and close supervision by the building contractor during construction.

2. Jack-arch roofs. Special precautions are required in earthquake areas. If a ring-beam has been constructed, the rolled steel joints (RSJs) should be firmly fixed to it. If not, each RSJ should be placed on a pad of concrete to spread the load over at least 300 mm. The RSJs should be held together so that they cannot separate, thereby allowing the brick arches to collapse on to the floor of the room below. This can be done by welding steel plates under the RSJs about 2.5 m apart.

3. Earth roofs. In addition to strengthening the walls of earth houses as described earlier, one further precaution should be taken if a flat roof of earth and pole construction is to be added. These roofs are very heavy, and it is vital that the roof

201

should be tied-in effectively to the walls or else the building will collapse rapidly under earthquake conditions, crushing the occupants. The way to protect the building and its users against this risk is to lay additional poles inside the walls to act as wall plates. Then the main poles, which should be cut a little longer than usual, can rest on them and should be firmly attached to the wall plates to tie the walls and roof together (Figure 12.5)

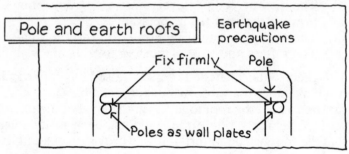

Figure 12.5

Fire precautions

It is very common for earthquakes to be followed by fires; fires which may cause more damage and loss of life than the earthquake itself. Following an earthquake, the fire-fighting service will be under great stress and their work may be made more difficult if pipes are broken and water is not readily available. It is wise to ensure that the possibility of fire damage is given priority in design, construction and maintenance decisions on buildings in earthquake areas. Three of the most important points to remember are:

1. Steel frames should be properly encased.
2. The ends of steel reinforcing bars should be hooked for maximum bond.
3. Fire precautions should be made more intensive to allow for delays in response to calls for fire-fighting.

Repairs

If a building has been damaged by an earthquake tremor but not totally destroyed, the damage must be properly diagnosed and thoroughly repaired. It is extremely dangerous simply to have a labourer plaster over all obvious cracks and repaint, since this may merely hide fundamental damage which could seriously

202

weaken the building and reduce its resistance to future stresses. The only responsible approach is to ensure that all damaged buildings are thoroughly examined by a qualified building surveyor, and also to ensure that funds are provided to finance any structural work that s/he states is crucial to the integrity of the building and the safety of its occupants.

CHAPTER 13

Towards a Maintenance Policy

What next?

What next? It is a reasonable question. The authors have attempted to cover a complex, underresearched, underfunded and generally neglected area under the three broad headings of Strategy, Management and Methods. But we recognize that this book alone, or for that matter any book, is not enough. In all but a few developing countries there is a desperate need for action, based upon a coherent and properly-funded maintenance policy. In turn this policy must be based on knowledge, both to define the nature and scale of the maintenance problem and to create an awareness among decision-makers that something can and must be done.

Hence this postscript. We believe that the neglect of building maintenance is so serious and so universal, that it demands intervention at national level. It also requires a recognition among donors and financing agencies that the provision of funding for maintenance is as beneficial, if not more so, than the provision of finance for spectacular new projects (which in turn will eventually add to the maintenance problem).

Starting at the beginning

The maintenance of buildings, and indeed, the maintenance of any physical asset, is a matter which must be considered long before the construction of a building starts. Each building has its own characteristics and will therefore have its own maintenance requirements. It is necessary to ensure that in designing and constructing a building, the system is suited to the user's needs, the maintenance costs can be contained from outset, and the life-cycle is optimized.

This is essentially the responsibility of the design team, who should feel accountable not only to their individual clients, but to the nation as a whole. Individual building owners and managers should also make arrangements not only to keep buildings in good structural condition, but to ensure that they keep the same performance standards as when the building was constructed. The diagram in Figure 13.1 emphasizes the role of

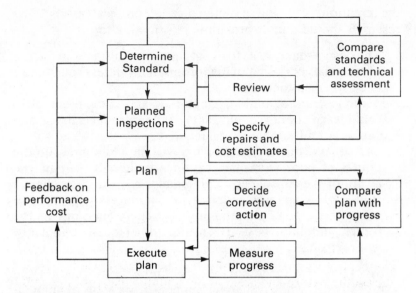

Figure 13.1 *Maintenance management process*

planning and control systems in the maintenance of buildings so as to maintain performance standards.

National responsibility

In order to prevent undue deterioration of its buildings there is a need to create a sense of national responsibility for building maintenance, based on an appreciation that maintaining existing assets is as respectable and worthwhile as creating new assets. Of course, governments can go beyond exhortation, and take direct action to encourage proper maintenance of buildings through financial assistance or legal requirements. One possibility mentioned earlier is the establishment of a specific rehabilitation fund which would allow property owners with modest funds access to money for repairs on reasonable terms. This could be funded by requiring every building owner to take an insurance policy or pay a levy towards the fund for purposes of repair and improvement. Coupled with this fund there could be statutory regulations requiring building inspection reports regularly, say every five years, to determine how much maintenance is required in order to ensure that the building keeps its value.

The need for research

In addition to the above measures, research is required at national level to provide basic data to all parties concerned with

205

the creation, use and maintenance of physical assets. The research should aim at providing information to:

1. The design team, so as to avoid repetitive mistakes in the use of materials or design of inappropriate facilities that create a need for maintenance.
2 Manufacturers of building materials and components who would learn about the durability of their products in use and eliminate undesirable characteristics.
3. Site supervisors and contractors who should appreciate the effects of poor workmanship on a building's life, and be aware of the consequent maintenance costs to their clients.
4. Building owners and maintenance managers who need to know the cost of maintaining particular buildings in the future and how best to ensure an adequate quality of workmanship.

Areas of research. In view of the lack of reliable information, the scope for worthwhile research is immense. Six areas of immediate interest are:

1. The service life of various building materials and components.
2. The influence of design on maintenance: how to design for minimum maintenance and how to design for maintainability.
3. Maintenance cost determinants.
4. Alternative approaches to the organization and administration of maintenance.
5. Information systems for building maintenance.
6. The role of maintenance in the construction industry and the scope for specialization.

How to go about it. Since there is such a dearth of research studies in the area of building maintenance, the Annex offers a case study drawn from research in Mombasa, Kenya between 1976 and 1983. This is not offered as a prototype to be followed precisely elsewhere, but to suggest a line of approach to those prepared to take the time and trouble to add to the stock of knowledge relating to building maintenance in their own country.

The objective. Research is not an end in itself. Nor is a maintenance policy, important as it is. The objective is both simple and clear, to improve the maintenance management process so as to provide building occupiers with a satisfactory working or living environment and building owners (frequently the community in one guise or another) with a satisfactory investment.

Building maintenance does not have to be haphazard. It is possible to budget and plan for routine maintenance as long as reliable information is available on the frequency of work-load by element and the implications. It is possible to save money by designing for minimum maintenance and maintainability, providing research findings are fed back to designers and manufacturers. Designers need hard facts on why particular items such as plumbing, decoration and roofs are frequently expensive to maintain. Factual information on costs would enable rational decisions to be made on the trade-off between a higher initial cost and the advantage of lower and less frequent repairs and maintenance over the life cycle of the building.

We therefore end with a plea for more research, since research remains the foundation upon which a full appreciation of the discipline of building maintenance should be founded.

Building Maintenance Research : an example

The following case study is drawn from research carried out in Kenya between 1976 and 1983 to determine the maintenance failure characteristics and costs of publicly-owned residential housing estates within some selected geographical regions. Only one region, that of the Mombasa Municipal Council, is described here. It is included as a guide to other researchers on some of the aspects that require examination in a study of this kind.

The study

Mombasa is an area with an extreme climate, which conditioned the need for and approach to maintenance by the authorities concerned. In other cases, one could envisage emphasis on atmospheric pollution (in an industrial city), socio-cultural factors or a shortage of key resources such as materials or skilled workers. With the emphasis on the effect of climatic conditions in mind, the study was made under the following headings:

Description of area and climate
Effect of climate on design
Effect of climate on structure and finishes
Source of data
Data base
Cost codes
Overall cost analysis
Building fabric cost analysis
Relative incidence of maintenance and repairs by elements.

Description of area and climate

Mombasa is the second largest town in Kenya, and is located in a hot and humid equatorial zone bordering the Indian ocean. It covers an area of 275sq.km, extends a maximum of 50km inland, and its altitude is less than 150m. The population density is in excess of 1,630 persons per sq.km. It has the largest harbour on the East Coast of Africa, north of Durban.

Both day and night temperatures in Mombasa are high, the mean maximum and minimum being 30.1°C and 23.4°C respectively, with a low diurnal range of 6.7°C. The mean annual relative humidities are high, being 93 per cent in the mornings and 66 per cent in the afternoons. The annual rainfall is 1,182mm with the highest precipitation of 235mm falling in May. There is an incidence of driving rain from April to October when Southeast monsoon winds cross the Indian Ocean.

Effect of climate on design
Due to the high humidity, natural ventilation is essential in the majority of buildings where air-conditioning cannot be economically justified. The prime objectives of design are accordingly to exclude solar heat, to facilitate air movement in and around the building, and to provide protection from the rains and other extreme climatic conditions. These aspects affect site planning, the house plan, structure and materials, as well as the location of openings such as windows and doors.

Several alternative design solutions are possible. Whatever choice is made, it will affect both the initial construction cost and the cost of maintenance, as well as the durability and economic life of the building. For instance, the need for air movement and ventilation may be met by generous spacing between houses or, if land is in short supply, increased building height in preference to increased ground coverage.

Effect of climate on structure and finishes
The extreme climatic conditions in Mombasa affect both the durability of buildings and the comfort of the occupants. Many materials are affected by high humidity and the high atmospheric salinity of the sea air. High humidity, for instance, encourages the corrosion of items such as galvanized corrugated iron sheets, steel pipes and window frames. Under continuous high humidities and temperatures, moulds and algae disfigure painted surfaces and cement-based products. Thus, in Mombasa, concrete walls, cement-mortar rendering, concrete tiles and asbestos sheets in exposed surfaces are susceptible to intense blackening.

The biological decay of timber and other materials is greatly encouraged by humid conditions. The driving rain during the Southeast monsoon winds not only damages external finishes, but if continuous over long periods leads to the saturation of outer walls and subsequent internal dampness. This may result in moisture movement which causes cracking in concrete blocks.

Mombasa's low latitude gives rise to a high ultra-violet content in solar radiation. This causes chemical deterioration in bituminous materials, and also causes paints to fade rapidly with resultant cracking and flaking.

Source of data
The data for this study was collected from about 8,000 conventional housing units on estates owned by four major public institutions in Mombasa. The data collected included maintenance costs, relative incidence of maintenance and repair requirements, and causes of maintenance problems. The ownership pattern was as follows:

Institution	Housing units
Municipal council	3,398
Central government	2,016
Railways corporation	1,412
Ports authority	1,157
	7,983

Data base
Data on maintenance costs was analysed for each element in each house owned by the institutions for the period 1974 to 1983, based on maintenance work instruction sheets, annual reports and abstracts of accounts. Each year's maintenance expenditure was raised to 1983 constant prices, using published residential building cost indices from the Central Bureau of Statistics. These figures represent the money equivalents of each year's expenditure for both labour and materials at constant prices.

The expenditure for each year was divided into the number of units on which the money was spent, and this was calculated for the study period of 10 years to arrive at an annual average maintenance cost per house or per room. Although there were variations between different houses owned by each institution, and between houses owned by various institutions, the data was analysed statistically, to obtain mean results as a guide for budgeting and the control of expenditure.

Cost codes
Items of expenditure were analysed according to the following cost-codes:

External and internal decoration
Plumbing and sanitary fittings
Electrical works
Roof repairs including chimneys and ceilings

Windows and doors
Floors and staircases
External walls and partitions
External site-works, including repair and cleaning of spaces
around and between buildings
Miscellaneous works not included in the above codes.

Overall cost analysis

The average annual expenditure per house (of about 100m^2) was
approximately US$100. When total maintenance costs for each
housing estate were considered, the expenditure on the building
fabric, general cleansing and grounds respectively was as
illustrated in Figure 1. The heading 'grounds' includes site-
works and estate roads which accounted in this case for less than
six per cent of total costs. Naturally, the latter costs vary with the
site slope, house layout and orientation, as well as site size and
density.

Cleansing accounting for nearly 18 per cent includes refuse
collection, street cleaning, bush clearing and gully or cesspit

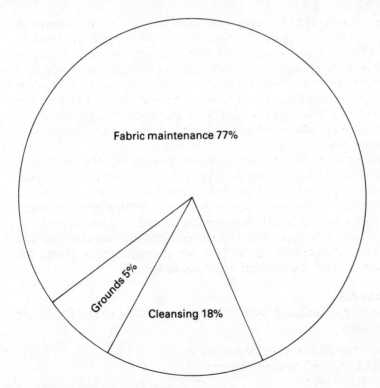

Figure 1 *Overall cost analysis*

211

emptying. The most expensive area of expenditure was related to repairs and maintenance of the building fabric accounting for nearly 77 per cent. The cost of maintaining the building fabric depended on the size of the building, the materials used in its construction, exposure to climatic conditions and user needs.

Building fabric cost analysis
Within the building fabric itself, costs were analysed by element. Figure 2 shows the overall analysis for all the houses for the whole period. The most expensive element was plumbing including water and sanitary fittings, followed by decoration and roofs. Plumbing fittings such as toilet cisterns, covers and seats, and water taps are particularly vulnerable to intensive use and abuse by occupants as often occurs in cases of overcrowding in rented apartments. The relatively high cost of decoration was affected by the adverse climatic conditions.

Roofs accounted for nearly 20 per cent of maintenance costs, and were boosted by the expensive replacement of finishes such as asphalt and bitumen on flat roofs, which are very vulnerable

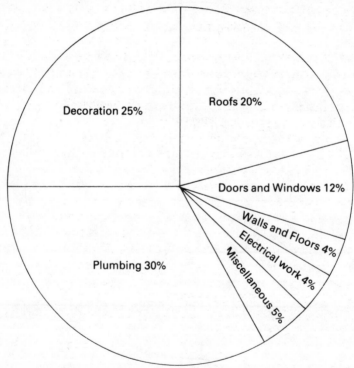

Figure 2 *Building fabric cost analysis*

to extreme climatic conditions. Where pitched roofs were used, timber decay at the verges and fascia boards was a frequent course of trouble. Timber doors and windows also suffered from exposure to the rains unless regularly repainted or recoated with varnish. Metal window frames were by no means trouble-free, and corrosion due to atmospheric salinity was frequently serious.

Relative incidence of maintenance and repairs by element
Figure 3 shows the relative frequency of repair works for each element as a percentage of all maintenance and repair works carried out during the period. The most frequent source of expenditure on repairs was plumbing, followed by decoration. They were also the most expensive elements to maintain.

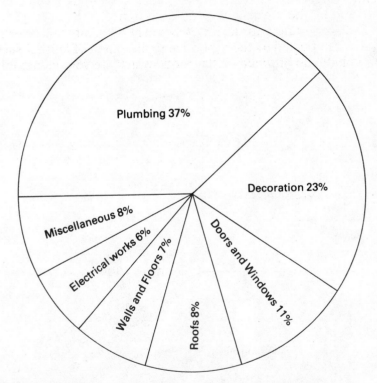

Figure 3 *Relative incidence of maintenance and repairs by element*